CONTACT IMPROVISATION

CONTACT IMPROVISATION

An Introduction to a Vitalizing Dance Form

Cheryl Pallant

McFarland & Company, Inc., Publishers

Jefferson, North Carolina, and London

All photographs are by John K. MacLellan

LIBRARY OF CONGRESS CATALOGUING-IN-PUBLICATION DATA

Pallant, Cheryl.
   Contact improvisation : an introduction to a vitalizing dance
form / Cheryl Pallant.
      p.   cm.
   Includes bibliographical references and index.

   ISBN-13: 978-0-7864-2647-8
   (softcover : 50# alkaline paper) ∞

   1. Improvisation in dance — History.   I. Title.
GV1781.2P35   2006
792.8 — dc22   2006014349

British Library cataloguing data are available

Cover photograph: Truth revealed in presence, Eric Ortega
and Burr Johnson.

Manufactured in the United States of America

McFarland & Company, Inc., Publishers
   Box 611, Jefferson, North Carolina 28640
   www.mcfarlandpub.com

To Carmen Beuchat

Contents

Contents

Acknowledgments

In my many years of doing Contact Improvisation, I have danced with over a thousand partners. Each of those dances, some with accompanying conversation, has been influential in helping me form the ideas that appear in this book. I thank my many dance partners for moving my body and my mind and provoking insight and laughter. Immeasurable gratitude goes to Steve Paxton for initiating the dance and to Nancy Stark Smith for ensuring its continuance. I thank both for lending their support on this project. I thank David Koteen for fanning the initial spark that became this book.

The text benefited greatly from the insightful critical comments at pivotal junctures from Jennifer Stanger, Allen Gay, and Elizabeth Hodges, each of whom deserves thanks. Gratitude goes to all who responded to my queries and those who agreed to be interviewed and photographed, especially jammers in Richmond, Virginia. Thanks to Sharon Russell and Rob Smith for poring over hundreds of photographs. A bounty of thanks goes to John MacLellan for skillfully capturing jam after jam with his lens and providing technical know-how. Thanks to the dance teachers who shared their lessons for use in this book.

Gratitude goes out to my many friends who have offered support, often over coffee, as this book expanded from notes into paragraphs into entire chapters. If Kevin Heffernan consumed coffee anywhere equal to the amount of encouragement he has provided, it would be years before he could sleep soundly. Thanks, Kevin, for sharing the moon and knowing where on the text to place your hands.

It is a delight to work with my agent Lilly Ghahremani. Thank you for your consistent clarity, shared vision, and work every step of the way.

Mr. Duffy lived a short distance from his body.
— James Joyce

To dance is to live.
— Isadora Duncan

Preface

Prior to my entering high school, a doctor diagnosed me with scoliosis and recommended I minimize all movement: no sports of any kind, no gym class, and no dancing. Though offered a metal back brace or cast to offset further spinal curvature, I opted for physical therapy. Several times a week, my thirteen-year-old body diligently performed a series of isometric exercises aimed at strengthening muscles, movements on one side mechanically duplicated on the other side. My doctor instructed me to sit straight, walk straight, and in essence, to hold my torso erect at all times, a regimen I carried out with dogged determination. In class or the hallway, high school teachers informed of my condition echoed the instructions when they caught me slouching or indulging in any wayward position.

Though no surgical knife ever cut my skin, whatever dance may have been edging its way into my life was successfully excised by a well-meaning medical establishment that offered me an improved, straightened body based on a mechanistic model that overlooked the value of individual differences and provided no insight into the body's personal workings. My curvature got no worse, but my abstention from moving led to spasms, chronic pain, and periodic momentary paralysis, symptoms my doctor explained with clinical detachment which would accompany me for life. "What do you expect with a condition like yours?" he offered with his eyes fixed on the folder containing my medical information.

A rebellious whim accompanied my attending college at Long Island University. I signed up for a dance class, Movement Improvisation, taught by Carmen Beuchat. Carmen left her native home of San-

1

tiago, Chile, entranced by what she'd heard about Merce Cunningham, whose style and approach to dance differed markedly from her extensive ballet training. Upon arriving in New York in the 1960s, she immersed herself in the experimental dance and theater of the period, working alongside Trisha Brown, Sylvia Whitman, and Robert Wilson, in performance on rooftops, the pond at Central Park, and stages in downtown Manhattan. Her classes reflected her newly adopted aesthetic. They also provided imaginative, playful, and challenging exercises for exploring the expressive body in motion. For me, the world's shutters opened, ushering in a feast of sensations and emotions connecting me firmly to my body and my surroundings. My rigid body with its limited range of motion reinforced by medical directives softened into the moving poetry of dance. Eager limbs ventured into previously off-limit directions — vertically, horizontally, diagonally. Undulations, stretches, twists, pulls, leaps — an entire repertoire of movement became available. In my trespass into unfamiliar spaces, the spasms and paralysis disappeared entirely, the pain vanishing also in subsequent years. Not surprisingly, I embraced dance as indispensable.

During one class, Carmen suggested I attend a performance of experimental dance at St. Mark's Church in New York City's East Village. The year was 1979, several years after Steve Paxton, founder of Contact Improvisation (CI), began exploring the form. That semester, he performed his solos at the university. Something about the ease in his movements, the seemingly effortless rising and falling of his arms, his crescendos, and what followed in their wake, intrigued me. I followed Carmen's suggestion, needing little convincing, although I had no idea what awaited me. The performance in New York marked my introduction to CI.

Paxton and Nancy Stark Smith were among several taking turns entering and exiting the floor, partnering in a dance with vigor and nonchalance. Their movements — fluid, bold, intricate, unpredictable, humorous, and sensual — astounded me. What amazing choreography, I thought. On learning that the movements were improvised, I returned to class excited to learn the form. To my dismay, Carmen was unable to teach the dance — something having to do with department pol-

2

icy — and I had to seek a workshop outside the school. I later attended classes with Smith, Danny Lepkoff, Andrew Harwood, Lisa Nelson, Simone Forti, David Appel, and others. Learning CI plunged me into a way of dancing that amazed, baffled, intrigued, delighted, and instructed me profoundly. Its impact has been ongoing and shows no sign of stopping any time soon.

So why a book on CI? In the years since its inception, very little has been written about this improvisational form, with two notable exceptions: Cynthia Novack's anthropological book, *Sharing the Dance,* which provides a comprehensive documentation of CI's history and contextualizes it among other dance forms; and the journal *Contact Quarterly,* which supplies a rich diversity of articles by CI practitioners investigating the form.[1] Since its inception in the early '70s, the dance has spread into a worldwide phenomenon practiced by professional dancers and enthusiasts alike. CI was once considered too avant-garde for most colleges, but today a growing number of dance departments offer classes in the form as a technique for training the body and a tool for generating choreography. Outside academia, in cities throughout the United States and abroad, in art centers, churches, or any sizeable space with a wood floor, groups meet regularly to practice CI and deepen movement exploration through informal gatherings called jams. Movements and principles of CI have been used by numerous choreographers like Bill T. Jones and Arnie Zane as well as throngs of jammers, or Contacters, many of whom may never step onto a stage in front of an audience. Professional dancers or not, all benefit from the practice, transforming their bodies and awareness and influencing culture. How can such an important phenomenon have been overlooked in the literature?

Dance, an ephemeral medium, gone once the dancer stills her body, often struggles to justify its existence and validity as art. Although strides have been made in recent years to document live work, video and photographs tend to flatten this three-dimensional art. Much work ends up neglected altogether. Furthermore, in a constant scramble to support their passion financially, many professional dancers rarely have the time or energy to step into the medium of words, which could help elevate the work on par with other media. Language, too, contains shortcomings, often proving imprecise in capturing the moment-to-moment changes in movement and consciousness; if not spoken or written carefully, words can misrepresent the form. Moreover, despite its respectability in music, jazz in particular, improvisation as a worthwhile pursuit in dance has often been suspect, even among those who might best profit from it. Where, some ask, is the craft or structure implying discriminating study? What is the art in moment-to-moment awareness? How can it be suitably packaged as a commodity? Lastly, modern Western society is largely a society uncomfortable with anything more than superficial attention brought to the body. A form with touch at its center, whose prime aim is not to appeal to an audience but to generate a spontaneous, authentic physical conversation between performers, has raised many an eyebrow, both within and outside dance communities. Many want to quickly categorize any display of sensuality as immoral and prurient or, more simply, as banal.

What does this book hope to achieve? As a voice in what I hope is an ongoing discourse on CI, I wanted to provide a more experiential perspective than Cynthia Novack's work, and offer my appreciation of and reflections upon the moving, feeling body. As a writer and dancer, I have often sought those who can articulate their experience, who can find expression not only through movement but also in words, one medium enhanced and furthered by the other.

I also hope to encourage readers to see CI for themselves. If you have never witnessed CI, find a place where you can watch it. Dare yourself to join in.

My insights, interests and experiences shape the primary perspective of this book. However, I wanted to include more than my own voice. To that end, I have woven into the text comments from fellow dancers, some new to the dance, others accomplished veterans. Much material was obtained through books, published and unpublished articles, interviews and emails.

This book aims to supplement ideas with practice. Following the narrative of each chapter are questions and exercises that CI teachers and I have used in class. The exercises are meant to shift attention toward awakening the body and mind, introduce skills, and inspire the dance. Some of these exercises are original; others have passed from teacher to teacher over the years, their originator lost in the sharing. The final chapter is devoted exclusively to exercises by several CI teachers in their own words and is an opportunity to learn different approaches to the same material. Altogether, the exercises are meant as complementary material to taking a class. CI cannot be learned through text alone. A body practice needs bodies.

Chapter 1, "The Creative Body: Source of a New Form," is devoted to the history of CI. Originating as a dance experiment at Oberlin College in Ohio in 1972, Contact Improvisation was presented for the first time by founder Steve Paxton in New York's Soho. He attracted the attention of fellow dancers who would prove instrumental in sharing the dance with colleagues and eager newcomers. This chapter charts the groundwork which gave birth to the dance, identifying influences and naming several key players like Nancy Stark Smith.

Chapter 2, "The Practicing Body: Contact Improvisation Fundamentals," lays out the principles that distinguish CI from other types of dance. Elements providing stylistic consistency include being guided by the contact point, remaining present, establishing centeredness, and following momentum. These elements enable dancers to maneuver around each other's bodies safely and generate an improvisation dance.

Chapter 3, "The Knowing Body: Self and Identity," explores ways in which identity is socially constructed and explains how CI helps to disassemble and reconstruct that identity with greater personal authenticity. This chapter addresses the perspective of the body as an object, vulnerable to inscription from a number of sources, and then highlights the importance of sensory awareness and unmediated, lived experience, not preconceived ideas or judgments, as a path to unfolding a more innate knowing and authenticity.

Chapter 5, "The Relating Body: Alienation and Orientation," examines the substantive exchange that occurs within the shared, intimate space of the dance in a culture that promotes individuality and its unintended by product, isolation. Presenting both a materialist perspective and an energetic one, this chapter exposes how touch makes boundaries porous, evoking a profound sense of connection.

Chapter 6, "The Tribal Body: Creating Community," unearths the ramifications of stepping outside social conventions into a counterculture. This chapter details the shared values of this global community, guidelines and decisions it has made, and some of the changes over the years.

Lastly, Chapter 7, "The Dancing Body: A Teacher's Sampler," collects a variety of exercises by CI teachers in their own words. The exercises reflect a few of the varied approaches used by teachers from across the United States and abroad.

Prologue

The body can relax, let go, take a vacation from trying so hard, or not at all.

Listen to the click of cartilage, the slap of skin, or the whisper of your will typically silenced by a shout.

Notice a part of your body for which you have no name, no history, no awareness. Not quite shoulder, not quite spine, but a previously unexplored space. Go there to see what lurks behind hard corners and soft contours.

Enter unseen corridors of your body as if there is no turning back, as if this moment is all you have.

Feel weight push into your stubbornness, your expectations, against your habit of always yielding to aggression or constantly fighting it. Try a new strategy. Breathe deeply. Watch with open attention. Watch for surprise.

Go because it feels better than what you did yesterday, because it feels like dessert without the added calories.

Go because you haven't been upside down in weeks. Or so incandescently upright.

The body can shed its evolutionary skin, secrete antiquated habits of survival that lean closer to extinction than animation.

Roll along the hill of a hip into the bloom of sensation. Plant seeds with every bend and gesture.

Invigorate. Pretend. Participate as best you can. Sniff the circumstances, the leg extending into view, the hand urging direction. Push against ribs. Pull an arm.

Play with the past and share the play. Watch time dissolve.

Consider every detail: hair, sweat, friction, levity, glee. Or ignore all that usually consumes your focus. Forget rules for the moment. Invent new ones.

Assert last night's dream, or a part of it, the part nearly forgotten. Follow the sound into the garden past the bench in the corner where weeds grow and the rabbit squeezes beneath the fence.

Look your partner in the eye. Note that many gates swing open and closed.

Don't wait. Encourage participation, penetrating breath, chi, prana, embodiment, an alchemical boil.

Find the pleasure in pain and the pain in pleasure.

Nudge blocked energy from slumber. Coax a muscle to stretch beyond its usual reach. Exhale quickly or ever so slowly. Yield to gravity's insistence and your partner's push.

Tend your body as if it were the body of a lover.

Follow your partner. Risk the road. Go down the untraveled paths of back or neck. Let bone graze bone. Fall into pools of flesh. Lounge in heat. Drink the elixir of expansion, the release within repose.

Go slow if your habit is fast, fast if your habit sluggish. Find the edge between comfort and discomfort, the familiar and the unknown. Balance there, however precariously.

Plod along like an elephant seal or dart with a leopard's stealth. Devolve into protozoa.

Find the current of your plasma. Feel the ceaseless divide of your cells.

Let your body call you back into yourself, into your most deeply embodied self. Land, dive, soar. Find the crumbs that lead back home.

1

The Creative Body: Source of a New Form

Art should be an affirmation of life, not an attempt to bring order ... but simply a way of waking up to the very life we are living, which is so excellent, once one gets one's mind and one's desire out of the way and lets it act of its accord.
— Jean Baudrillard

If I can't dance I don't want to be part of your revolution.
— Emma Goldman

Two dancers move from separate areas of the dance floor to occupy the same space. Feet are bare, cotton sweatpants and a T-shirt fit loosely. One's elbow grazes the other's belly. The belly expands, prompting the elbow to straighten and the arm to thrust outward. This movement provokes another as both bodies roll on available surfaces — the back, a shoulder, a thigh — playing with resistance, pliancy, momentum, gravity, the pressure of flesh against flesh. At any moment, the dance may slow or speed up, reveal athletic prowess or tenderness. So begins a duet of Contact Improvisation, every dance a fresh combination of chance and openness to motion, a partnered improvisational dance that relies on bodies moving together with no set moves other than an awareness of their dynamic exchange of touch.

Begun in 1972, CI challenges easy definition. In addition to identifying it as experimental dance, practitioners have called it art-sport, folk dance, meditation, therapy, play, and a technique for choreography. All of these identities bear merit. However, when dancer Steve

Paxton founded the form, his intention was to explore the specific movements arising from the pairing of bodies in motion; he was investigating the perception and performance of dance. He recalls, "When we started, we didn't know what we were making or where precisely it was going. We had to leave room for its organic development rather than where we wanted it to go.... CI is dance primarily between two people who remain in touch but dance independently, creating a third entity between them. This third entity is CI."[1]

This distinctive partnered dance relies exclusively on the abilities of the dancers to remain in touch with their own and another's body improvisationally. Dancers find ways to pivot, roll, balance, and fall, following sensation and the momentum of their moving bodies, without a predetermined plan or musical accompaniment.

BACKGROUND

Paxton commonly uses the language of physics — words like momentum, gravity, chaos, and inertia — to describe CI's movements. His choice of metaphors results from what he perceived in the '70s as a gap in dance training. No language suitably explained what went on between couples. Additionally, dancers rarely discussed partnering. "Appalling barren" is how he referred to the absence of partnering analysis in modern dance and ballet. "Although you might have another twenty-five people in the room with you," he explains, "you kept a certain distance from everybody so you wouldn't be kicking them. You learned technique as an isolated person, and then you crossed the floor, perhaps even in groups, but always with distance."[2] This omission became territory for investigation.

Paxton's creative explorations were part of larger shifts. The 60s marked a time of great social and political change. Cultural ideals were shifting dramatically, with expanded rights for women and blacks. Eastern religions firmly landed on Western shores, and the New Age Movement was flourishing. Great artistic inquests earmarked this period. In dance and theater, folks like Deborah Hay, Robert Rauschenberg,

Simone Forti, Yvonne Rainer, Meredith Monk, and groups like the Grand Union, The Judson Church Dance Theatre, and The Wooster Group actively challenged expectations, blurring boundaries between audience and performer, art and life, one art discipline bleeding into another. With Happenings instigated by Allen Kaprow, events at North Carolina's Black Mountain College, Situationists, and a vital art scene in New York's Soho, the art world was rife with rule benders and form blenders, a virtual art laboratory.[3] Dance training broadened to include somatic methods developed by people like F.M. Alexander and Moshe Feldenkrais. Paxton, who performed with Jose Limon, Merce Cunningham, The Judson Project, and Grand Union, among others, danced on fertile ground.

In January 1972, Paxton, then part of Grand Union, a collective of dance theater improvisers that included Barbara Dilley (then Lloyd), Trisha Brown, Yvonne Rainer, Douglas Dunn, David Gordon, and Nancy Peck (then Green), were invited for a three-week arts residency at Oberlin College in Ohio. Paxton had been exploring commonplace movements like walking and standing, a study that helped him break down the distinction between customary dance phrasing and pedestrian, or ordinary, movements. Choosing to work with men only, he used his visit to explore extremes of orientation and disorientation. The investigation resulted in "Magnesium," now considered the seminal dance for CI. In this work, eleven men repeatedly fling themselves at one another, colliding, sliding, and falling onto a cushioned mat. One of the students watching was Nancy Stark Smith, and she approached Paxton with her interest in working with him, should he decide to work with women on the material presented in "Magnesium." Trained in sports yet disheartened by its competitiveness, she was drawn to the physical rigor of "Magnesium." Several months later, Paxton invited colleagues as well as students from his guest residencies at Oberlin College, Bennington College, and University of Rochester, among them Smith, Curt Siddall, Nita Little, Mary Fulkerson, Danny Lepkoff, and Laura Chapman, to meet in New York City for a week of rehearsals followed by a week-long performance at the John Weber, a Soho art gallery. Says Paxton, "We worked at the Weber and showed our progress — and lack of it — to the public because I had a strong feeling this was something that should be seen from the beginning, that it was going to progress."[4] The show marked the first time the dance was referred to as Contact Improvisation.

Reaction to the Weber showing and subsequent performances that summer was mixed and provided little indication that the dance would catch on to the degree it did. In part, this had to do with its presentation. No program announced names of dances, nor were there rows of chairs separating dancers from the audience. Without a traditional proscenium, audience members filtered in and out of the space, often en route to a number of Soho galleries. The dancers casually took turns standing on the sidelines and entering the dance space with no set cues other than an impulse. No one applauded; however, the structure of the performance didn't encourage it either. About the reaction to the Weber showing and subsequent performances at colleges, museums, and dance studios, Paxton recalls, "People seemed intrigued to see a form of improvisation, a coherent process with a goal. Improvisation was a word with only a general definition at that point in dance, though in theater, processes had already been found and tried."[5]

If the dance were to evolve beyond the abrasive and disjointed collisions in "Magnesium," Paxton recognized he had to teach his partnered dance, with its Aikido rolls, falls, and format, and its moment-to-moment awareness, to fellow dancers. Many of New York's downtown dancers as well as his students were eager participants, especially Smith, who viewed hour upon hour of video of practices and performances, helping Paxton to deepen his understanding and acquire a vocabulary for the dance. By 1975, the group ReUnion formed, with Paxton, Smith, Curt Siddall, and Nita Little (and later including Danny Lepkoff, Lisa Nelson, David Woodberry, and others), to perform and teach the dance annually on the West Coast; different configurations of dancers and ad hoc groups presented the work on the East Coast and elsewhere.

Aiming for a consistent but not closed form, Paxton described CI in a *Drama Review* article in 1975 as a work in process which contained six essential elements: attitude; sensing time; orientation to space; orientation to partner; expanding peripheral vision; and muscular development, which includes centering, stretching, taking weight, and increasing joint action. He explains, "Each party of the duet freely improvises with an aim to working along the easiest pathways available to their mutually moving masses. These pathways are best perceived when the muscular tone is lightly stretched to extend the limbs.... Within this flexible framework, the shape, speed, orientation, and personal details of the relationship are left to the dancers who, however, hold to the ideal of active, reflexive, harmonic, spontaneous, mutual forms."[6]

Though CI was a new type of dancing in many regards, he considered it a composite of already existing forms such as wrestling, jitterbug, Aikido, gymnastics, and modern dance. Says Paxton, "I feel we have invented nothing; rather, specified a way of activity that is exclusive of the *aims* of other duet forms."[7]

As one of the more consistently visible CI teachers over the years, Smith has been asked repeatedly by numerous Contacters what it was like to be part of the dance since its beginning, a question accompanied with the mistaken assumption that the novelty and grandeur of the dance prompted alerts about its birth sent out to every corner of the dance world. Smith downplays the impact entirely and finds it amusing to consider that "CI could have been a piece that Steve Paxton made in 1972 which lasted two weeks, one week of rehearsal and one week of performance, and then he went on to his next idea.... All the dancers, too, went on to their next idea ... but the coherence as a form and a developing thing would have been lost. There were certain key decisions made along the way to try to protect it or encourage its growth as an entity rather than bar people from using it."[8]

PASSING THE DANCE

A key initial decision, not to retain exclusive claim to the dance, helped its spread. Paxton was less interested in maintaining control than he was in seeing where the form would go on its own. He considered copyrighting the dance, a concern which grew from hearing stories of injured dancers. Dancers were imitating the movements, throwing and catching, for instance, without learning how to work with the fundamentals of sensitivity, touch, and gravity. Going so far as to draft the papers for copyright, he wanted to protect the integrity of the dance and prevent it from being used recklessly. Ultimately he decided against trademarking the work, preferring ongoing dialog instead. The result: Without first getting permission from Paxton, those who learned the dance could perform it, incorporate aspects of it into their choreography, and teach it, even with variations, enabling dancers to tie it into their own movement experience. Even today, he refuses to claim the terrain mapped out by CI as his own. He doesn't command that only an elite few lead the Contact brigade. One needn't go through years of training at a Paxton Institute to learn the dance and obtain CI teaching accreditation. Instead, anyone who feels significantly skilled can teach or perform.

Within the first few years during the '70s, jams cropped up in major cities around North America — in Boston, Berkeley, San Francisco, Montreal, Vancouver, and Toronto, and later in places like Putney, Vermont, Washington D.C., Minneapolis, Seattle, and Juneau, Alaska, and soon after in Denmark and England. Largely, teaching and performance opportunities dictated its spread. More and more college dance, physical education, and therapy departments with sympathetic and curious faculty grew interested in the form and offered invitations to the growing number of dancers earning their living from CI.

Over the years, there have been many performances of CI by long-time dancers and bold newcomers; however, CI occurs primarily through weekly informal gatherings called jams. Jams typically include a warm-up and dancers rotating in duets, trios, quartets and so forth, sometimes in a slightly more formal structure, a round robin, where alternating partners dance in the center of the room while others look on from the periphery and await their turn to dance. Jams, more participatory than performance driven, some with musical accompaniment, are peopled by anywhere from a handful to several dozen novice and highly skilled dancers. Large annual jams, such as Breitenbush in

Oregon, the East Coast Jam in West Virginia, and the European Contact Improvisation Teachers Exchange (ECITE, at a different location across Europe each year), attract as many as 150 participants from a number of countries and have been instrumental in exposing more and more people to the dance.

CI has proliferated due to these jams, classes offered privately and through universities, and the establishment of *Contact Quarterly*, a newsletter established by Smith in 1975, which expanded into a journal a few years later and continues as a biannual today. Founded to encourage dialog about CI and related practices, the journal also functions as an essential tool enabling CI practitioners to stay in touch with each other; at the end of each issue is a list of addresses and phone numbers, upcoming classes, jams, and improvisation festivals. Contacters traveling from one city to another can readily find the location and time of a jam. As a result, what began with a handful of practitioners blossomed into a worldwide phenomenon. Jams and classes occur in numerous cities throughout North America and abroad, in South America, Europe, Asia, and Africa, with notably high populations of Contacters in Germany and Argentina.

Paxton's founding of CI pointed a finger at one's own body and another's, an act with profound personal and societal implications. Of utmost significance and the trait that sets it apart form all other dances is its emphasis on a moving yet continuous, improvisational touch, the contact point, an unmistakable space that joins two dancers together intimately. Of comparable importance, the dance is egalitarian, either partner free to lead or follow, its on-the-spot decisions challenging practitioners physically and psychologically.

Given that they were working within the dance field, it's no surprise that dance companies like Mirage, ReUnion, Mangrove, and Contraband, comfortable with experimentation, were some of the first to embrace CI. By virtue of their training and desire for distinction, dancers and choreographers typically venture into new aesthetic and kinesthetic experiences. As a testament to its staying power, however, subsequent generations of dancers, such as Arnie Zane and Bill T. Jones, Bebe Miller, Stephen Petronio, and David Dorfman, and more recently

Jayne Bernasconi and Brian Buck, integrate CI principles into their choreography, be it how they partner, work with balance and support, or take creative risks. CI has seeped into the vocabulary available to modern dance and shows no sign of disappearing anytime soon.

BEYOND THE DANCE FLOOR

Significantly, individuals outside professional dance embrace the work as well, partly because of Paxton's democratic reign. Experienced dancers move alongside newcomers, who move alongside computer analysts, who move alongside carpenters, who move alongside therapists. Whereas much dance is available primarily to slender, lithe bodies with innumerable hours of dance training, typically the sole harbingers of dance, CI practitioners welcome all onto the floor, including individuals with a range of body types — large, petite, differently-abled, aged. No one is discouraged from entering the dance.

CI has spun off into a multitude of directions — into areas other than dance, including meditation, play, therapy, recreation, exercise, sport, disability. Though its use continually gets adapted, it has not abandoned its original premise as a partnered movement form, a physical dialogue. Says Contact teacher Danny Lepkoff, "Contact Improvisation speaks for the belief that the realm of the organic body movement is limitless and rich in the possibilities of one's self, one's being."[9]

Paxton's lack of proprietorship extends also to an absence of artistic expectations, and the result has been CI's proliferation into areas he never conceived of initially. Consistent with the attitude of improvisation, he fully admits an openness to its progress from the beginning: "I have withheld that kind of thinking for this entire time. I want to see where *it* wants to go.... I think if I had a goal or if I projected a goal, I might inhibit it. So I want it to do what it does."[10]

For Contacters, the body is a vast resource, no mere concept safely quarantined by thought. Much more than cognitive play, CI demands visceral responses. When dancers spend innumerable hours pressed by the weight of one another, bodies transform. Muscles awaken and enlarge, weight shifts, bones strengthen, posture shifts. As the body changes, so too does one's thinking, mind and body inextricably entwined.

QUESTIONS

- What is the difference between warming up and improvising?
- How does skill get in the way of improvising?
- When is your dance a vital movement exchange, and when are you repeating moves out of convenience or because you've witnessed them done by others?
- How does gravity influence motion and motion influence emotion?
- How do you enhance spatial and kinesthetic awareness?
- In what ways do your movements shift when you relax your jaw, your shoulders, or focus on your breath?
- Where does the dance begin? Where does it end?

EXERCISES

Warm-up with Breath

Sit in a comfortable position. Invite breath into your body. Focus attention on your lungs. Imagine their shape as they take in air and notice, too, the change to your ribs. How do your lungs release air? Slow and smooth, haltingly, or quickly? Note distinctive features of the billowing and contracting of each breath. What shape do they take? Does your belly, neck, or any other part of your body move?

Let your lungs enlarge further with air. Fill your entire rib cage with breath, enough to occupy your back completely. Notice any shift in temperature. Adjust your position as needed. If you get dizzy, return to normal breathing.

Send breath to the center of your pelvis. Widen your base for support. Stretch your spine upward. Fill the entire cavity of your pelvis. Let breath emanate from that center. What is its natural motion? Does it percolate, swirl, ripple?

Send breath to areas distant from your lungs. Aim for your organs, bone marrow, limbs, face. See your body as spherical with breath rising outward from the center. Let the motion of breath move you. Start with small, incremental movements and gradually magnify them. See the motion as a solo dance. Embellish the expansions and contractions.

Notice how movements ignite awareness. Look for stretches, compression, relief, tension, heat, scents, images, hums. Let your body respond to itself. If something specific like a pain in your knee captures your attention, stick with it. Send breath there. Make it your dance partner. Respond to it in movement until something else comes into focus.

Whatever has been your tempo, alter it, slowing, speeding up, or alternating between the two. Let movement unfold from movement. Exaggerate the motion. Let motion in an arm travel to the spine or a leg. This is your personal current. Go along for the ride.

Variation: Begin by lying down. As you welcome more and more movement into your body, abandon this position for sitting up or traveling across the space.

Evolutionary Development

Begin on your side in a fetal position, eyes closed. Imagine yourself as a few-week-old embryo. You float as soft tissue in a permeating amniotic sea that periodically rocks and jostles you. Enjoy the gentle waves. Develop distinguishable legs, arms, and internal organs. Grow until you are ready to birth yourself. Let the delivery into a welcoming world be easy. Greet it with a momentous breath.

Roll onto your belly, arms folded by your side. Let your mouth and tongue be loose. Pucker your lips; listen for sounds. Open your eyes, but only softly focus on light and shapes. Clench your fingers and toes; release them. Take time as an infant to discover the floor, light, shapes. Eventually attempt a crawl. Move from one developmental stage to the next. Attempt standing and then walking.

Recognize other "children" in the room with you. Interact with them, making simple sounds or going over to them. Wonder at what you encounter. Play, explore, feel fear, joy, or any other emotion. Indulge your curiosity. Be impulsive and mutable, your body soft and responsive. Allow contact with a fellow "child" and let a dance happen.

Variation: Partner only when you reach preadolescence or older.

Variation: Begin as an elder and devolve back into a youth or infant.

Supported Warm-up

Engage in your usual warm-up; however, situate yourself beside a partner. As you proceed with your process, make periodic contact with your partner. Graze his or her skin. Rest on a leg. Deepen a stretch using your partner's resistance. Use your partner as a prop. Use the support his or her proximity provides to allow you to awaken to your warm-up habits. What typically gets neglected? What regularly receives attention? Repeatedly return to the present moment. What is new here? What is unique?

Variation: Both you and your partner warm-up together, using each other as props. Navigate the differences.

2

The Practicing Body: Contact Improvisation Fundamentals

Say you stumble or bump into somebody ... do they take off any points?
— Anthony Fugard

When a dancer is fully engaged, it is often difficult to remember all the moves and what led to them. Spotty recall poses little problem in performing the dance, as long as the dancer can return fresh to improvisation upon entering the floor with collaborators. But gaps in remembering make teaching CI a challenge. How can you instruct others if you retain only a part of what you just finished, its description similarly elusive?

When he began teaching CI at Vermont's Bennington College in the early '70s, Paxton focused on rolling and falling techniques from Aikido. These techniques helped explain effective and safe ways for bodies to rotate and land on available surfaces. With rolling and falling only two movements among numerous possibilities within the dance, a question early Contacters asked was not only what movements constituted the dance and provided it an identity distinct from other dance forms, but also how to teach it to fellow dancers. In the decades since CI began, collaboration and discussions with fellow dancers have been crucial to that end. Analyzing and discussing the dance helped fill in memory gaps and break down into separate components what otherwise appeared as continuous movement, increasing everyone's understanding. Such discussions allowed the original dancers of CI to teach both the subtleties of touch as well as bold moves like flying and falling.

MAKING CONTACT

What then are the guidelines of CI? What distinguishes the dance from tango or any other modern dance? As its name implies, a central feature of Contact Improvisation is physical contact. Touch is essential to the dance, its lodestar; dancers share a constantly moving point of touch. A heel meets a shoulder, or belly with back, hip with hip — these and innumerable constantly changing combinations provide possible touch sites. No one site or combination is prioritized above another.

Vital information about the direction and quality of the dance exchanges through this dynamic touch site. Here information about weight, energy, strength, balance, and sensitivity relays back and forth between partners. In place of words, the close proximity of bodies sharing weight and skin, bony and soft surfaces, firm and slack muscles all provide an endless stream of information about the physical condition of the dancers and where the dance can go. Tired or frail bodies may quickly fold down to the floor or maintain a feathery touch as they sashay across the floor. Muscled dancers with steady balance may ignite a high speed dance where the point of contact shifts swiftly.

There is no right or wrong site of contact, but dancers must establish a physical connection and stay in touch with one another for the dance to proceed. If a point of contact is never established, the dance loses its distinction as CI. A feathery touch may dominate one dance, but a consequent dance may evolve out of a firmer touch and sharing of weight, one body leaning emphatically into the other with ample opportunities for pivots and lifts.

The contact point roves the body's contours finding new combinations continuously, impelled by gravity's pull, by a slide or a wedge, by the press and play of firm and feeble flesh. A body angling into

Establishing a contact point: Corrine Mickler and Brandon Crouder.

another sets all sorts of rhythmic and erratic actions into motion. Bodies spiral and roll around one another, pour weight into the other, limbs and torsos shifting, relaxing, stretching, following, bending, releasing. One movement prompts the next. Toe, head, elbow, belly. To the floor tumbling, leapfrogging, squatting. Rising into the air onto the shoulders, slipping to the waist, to the floor, into a handstand. An expression of joy, conflict, dread, or humor. All the while, the contact point, a benign irresolute guide, directs partners who move together, yielding, asserting, influencing, and being influenced. Partners discover pathways around the body's landscape in an energetic mix of effort and effortlessness.

Consider your partner a jungle gym from which your body climbs, swings, slips, spirals, and leans. You may hoist your entire weight onto a sturdy surface, lace your limbs around vertical and horizontal planes, or dangle from your carefully placed ankles. Jungle gyms tend to be securely anchored into the ground, reliable in their ability to withstand shifting weight without coming up from the ground. Here the analogy ends. However tall or firm in balance, your partner is not made of metal, is not bolted into the floor, and, of utmost significance, *will* move. This mobility does not make your partner unreliable. Rather, your partner's movement and shifts in balance play an integral role in the push and play of the dance. Your partner's movement dynamic interacts with your own, the combination manifesting as particulars of the dance. The continual movement makes attending to the contact point all the more important. As bodies stand, twist, or turn upside down, one's world topsy-turvy, the contact point orients partners, points toward navigable surfaces and provides essential information about how to maneuver. Though it changes constantly, the contact point is the central channel joining partners, a fulcrum that supports complementary motion.

In establishing a point of connection, especially if I've not danced with my partner before, I tend at first to move more slowly than I might with a more familiar partner. We may establish contact at the shoulders and lean incrementally into each other. As I give more and more of my weight to my partner, I find out what amount of support is available. Does my partner stiffen? Does she shake from the strain of holding me? How firm is her balance? Is she retreating from or pressing into my touch? Typically, the sharing of weight ignites a series of movements. My upper back rolls across her back. Our heads meet. She tips further toward me, and I scoot below her, my back to her chest. I lift her with my pelvis, and we travel a few feet across the floor. She slides off, turns, and her pelvis now presses into mine. I lean back, belly up. Wherever our flesh meets, I seek out the center of her balance and aim to maintain my own, allowing the points of contact to guide our dance, to keep us in touch and lead us into developing a dance.

At all times, my aim is staying in a touch relationship with my partner, to release weight toward her and the floor, and to respond to

Rolling the contact point along the back: Cheryl Pallant (*top*) and Steve Bradley-Bull.

sensation. We are not operating from known routines nor carrying out someone's carefully arranged composition. Gone, also, is the attempt to make the dance look "good," to appeal or communicate to the watchful gaze of an observer, important criteria for choreographed dance which depends heavily on being viewed. Noting the absence of appealing to the tastes of an audience, dancer and writer Sally Banes says that CI makes the audience "obsolete." With CI, the traditional audience-performer relationship undergoes a dramatic shift. The internal experience takes precedence over the dance's appearance to an outsider. The physical exchange between performers takes priority over anyone on the sidelines. Whether dancers fly exuberantly on another's shoulders or fearfully slide off, point or curl their toes, the value and character of the dance is determined solely by those performing it. What matters is the mutual flow of sensation, the kinetic conversation between the dancers involved, not its entertainment or aesthetic worth to an outsider's critical eye.

IMPROVISING WITH THE PRESENT MOMENT

CI requires that practitioners learn movements that go beyond a superficial or premeditated sculpting of the body into sequential shapes. Movements arise from a reflexive relationship with a partner, not a preconceived ideal. A distinguishing feature equal in importance to maintaining a contact point and an inherent challenge to the dance is its

An easy connection starting the dance: Brandon Crouder and Kenika Kiante Canty.

26

improvisational structure. No one tells the dancer before heading onto the floor what moves to perform, in what sequence, for how long, and with whom. Like a writer's blank page, the dance floor, though it may already be peopled by fellow dancers, remains unscripted.

The unknown looms like an insistent, unanswered question. The dance may dissolve after five minutes or last an hour, may include one partner or several, may exhibit athleticism or traverse a variety of physical and psychological terrains. Props or sounds may be incorporated impromptu into a phrase to amplify a gesture or mood, or an instruction blurted, followed, perhaps, by its abrupt abandonment. Grace, comfort, awkwardness, skittishness, or any other quality arising in the moment may dominate or merely accent the dance. Typically, the dance is performed without music.

The particulars of CI are determined moment to moment, partners allowing the smooth or bumpy course of the dance to emerge on the spot. Continuously, Contacters note the instantaneous occurrences of their intermingling bodies. They follow sensation's interplay with gravity, impulse, momentum, and each other. They enter a mutually reflexive, living relationship with their surroundings, responding to a host of sensory stimuli. The muscle, tendon, and joint movements of kinesthetics and the more inward proprioceptive prompts are reacted to as they surface and are dealt with in split-second, frequently unconscious decisions. Sensately alert to the constantly changing environment and moving contact point, the Contacter is free to move any number of directions with no prespecified qualities. The resulting movement phrases may look the same as last week's; more likely, they'll take on a new character altogether. Shake an arm, toss the head back, pivot off a partner's hip. Or not.

PATH AS GOAL

There is no predetermined goal for which to aim, no premeditated resolution, idea, or feeling to demonstrate, no message or meaning to convey. Warm up your body, engage in a solo dance, and move to a section of the floor where encounters with fellow dancers are likely. Breathe. Stretch. Note the arrival and retreat of bodily phenomena. How do you engage with any of it? Let whim determine the focus of your attention and with whom you partner in a dance. Or be direct and deliberate and seek out a specific type of dance and partner.

For some, the absence of definite steps intimidates. When else are we given such leeway to be so unscripted? When else do we attend so closely to the coming and going of our breath and the existential baggage carried each time the lungs expand and contract with life? Typically, routines and habit infiltrate the day, activities such as brushing our teeth, going to work, and preparing dinner, all of which we perform more or less in the same way day after day. Unless we're vigilant, routine can dull us to the births in each moment and snare us into complacency and a reinforcement of the quotidian. Improvisation encourages an open-ended approach and welcomes impulsiveness. It invites perceiving anew. It recognizes time as elastic and our being as limber and variable. It promotes opportunities to break away from usual standards and restrictions, to step outside familiar patterns, to look afresh and come up with wholly new responses to our living environment. It lets us notice the shallowness or depth of our breath and how we withdraw from or seek out specific relationships. It reveals to what extent we flow with or resist the dancing physics of existence. Ruth Zaporah, founder of the improvisatory Action Theater, relies on improvisational principles similar to those of CI and recognizes that a "spontaneous mind works from an unencumbered perspective. To do this ... we look at experience. We take it apart. We look at expression. We take it apart. We look at our behavior, our habits. We take them apart. Then we experiment with putting the parts back together in unfamiliar ways."[1] Improvisation means that one moment we extend a leg by leading with our heel and later initiate a similar movement from our hip. Improvisation means that in one dance we catch a body as it hurls toward us, seconds later finding ourselves in the throw of someone's arms. Improvisation means that when we find ourselves in the same position in a consequent dance, we may respond to the hurling body instead by stepping aside and offering a hand for a soft landing.

To be goalless in the dance pushes us away from expected results and promotes openness to the ongoing arrival of sensation, the foundational information that links us with the now of our being and surroundings. Focus turns to our immediate interactions, our experiential engagement, the body sweating, pressing, stuttering in relationship with the floor, moving bodies, a spider, a dust particle, or anything which may be in the studio and our field of awareness.

Improvisation grants permission to incorporate the unconscious and the impetuous, the ugly and the graced, the predictable and the unforeseen into the dance; action need not be planned nor understood. Movements and qualities emerging from the mysterious underground spring — suddenly, briefly, forcefully, or comically — converge upon the dance, become its very fodder. We suddenly find ourselves in the sensory wilderness of the body. It is no longer adequate to maneuver based on thought and analysis alone, which distances us from the immediacy of sensory experience. A dancer may pursue a safe, well-traveled road along an arm or attempt an untried path along the sole of a foot. Instant visceral responsiveness and an animal-like acumen grab center stage and capture attention, provoking action. The richness of every moment assumes monumental importance.

It is not uncommon to respond to being set free in the body's wildness with confusion, discomfort, even fear. Though some may initially reach the delight poet Mary Oliver describes in her poem "Wild Geese" as letting "the soft animal of your body love what it loves,"[2] those new to dance and new to an emphasis on bodily awareness may find dizziness, tumult, and disorientation lurking at every turn and repose. After learning what is expected of them, students in the first day of my university CI classes often debate whether to drop out rather than face and understand their aversion. It's common to push what's uncomfortable and unfamiliar aside rather than embrace it out of curiosity. Habits, and the ease associated with them, don't easily relinquish governance to the squirms and the fleeting, seemingly idiosyncratic events summoning us from the margins. Yet the seed of many opportunities hide in coarse, even thorny casings, and always by the third class meeting, these very students are the same ones who don't want the class to end.

Our usual mode is to transfer sensation from its pure, indefinite state into a defined experience. A movement makes us "queasy." We say the movement is "good" or "smooth" or any other term that approximates the experience. We name the movement, categorize it, conceptualize it, and judge it one way or another. We make what is formative and foreign into something understandable, knowable, and governable. We slice the continuum of living into episodes and perspectives. Rather than float on the prods and pokes of sensation and leave them as formative, we assign meaning and establish a relationship to them within a frame of reference, essential responses, for the most part, to a life well lived. Yet improvisation favors dancers who focus on sensate awareness, welcoming the pauses and impulsiveness without manufacturing the bubbles, nudges, and glimmers into a conceptual product or judgment. Improvisation encourages returning to an attitude of a beginner's mind and discovering the world without prejudice, moving in ways that may unnerve us initially. It may lead to a shoulder stand upon your thigh, my legs afterward wrapping around your neck, you grabbing my waist to lift me right side up, momentarily blurring the horizon and my proclivity to be in control and know where I am at all times. The invitation from your hands and the fall of my weight assert their own agendas. Always the intention is remaining in the flow of the dance.

Returning to the building blocks of experience comes with its share of delights and challenges. Familiar behaviors and usual expectations turn unfamiliar, and when assumptions are compromised, comfort levels tend to drop, leading to confusion and uncertainty, feelings that may coincide with liminal states. These states are neither inherently bad or good, but reveal our vulnerability and predilection for familiarity. Smith embraces disconcerting states, finds in them the very gems of the dance. She says, "Where you are when you don't know where you are is one of the most precious spots offered by improvisation. It is a place from which more directions are possible than anywhere else. I call this place the 'Gap.' The more I improvise, the more I'm convinced that through the medium of these gaps — this momentary suspension of reference point — comes the unexpected and much sought after 'original' material."[3]

30

An important distinction in improvisation is that however liberating and free it appears, the arrangement, or lack thereof, is not carte blanche, an exemption from guidelines altogether. Any improvisation comes with a degree of structure, a new set of instructions. As Paxton readily concedes, "To be 'free' of circumstance only means to be in another."[4] An improvised dance may have a set beginning, but no predetermined end. It may situate a performer in a scene, yet leave no further instruction. It may provide guidelines about the use of objects in the room and a chosen feeling, but leave open character and timing. Few or ample instructions, a chance operation or a more deterministic approach, improvisational structures come as varied as the imaginations of those involved. For CI, dancers are expected to remain in physical contact with one another, breaking it only periodically.

If there is a goal for CI, it may be to remain present, to be mindful of the body, to keep an ongoing, unmediated awareness cued to sensate experience. Contacters note their own bodily experiences while staying simultaneously sensitive to their partner's, recognizing, for instance, when muscles soften or tense, if a partner can sustain weight, or how to avoid crushing a knee or ankle. Aspiring to be free of specific expectations, dancers constantly listen to and respect not only their own body but also their partner's. One does not impose an unwelcome experience upon another, manifesting, perhaps, as increasing speed or giving full weight. Essentially, dancers discern the difference between allowable, sustainable movements and unwelcome, unendurable ones, such differences changing day to day and partner to partner. No terrain is off-limits, yet if one partner feels overwhelmed, the dance will surely come to a quick, unsatisfying end.

LISTENING TO MOTION

Listening, a term regularly used in CI, is key to a mutually satisfying dance. Listening, according to CI's metaphorical use of the word, refers to paying attention to all the sensory occurrences arising from touch, from the play of weight as partners move through space, and

Gazing inward: Lynda Fleet Perry.

from the event of one body encountering the presence of another. Listening refers to noticing stimuli not only within oneself but also from another; refining this ability comes through repeated trials. As the complexity of the body reveals its secrets, Contacters eventually discover the existence of worlds upon worlds.

In listening, partners pay attention to the ongoing fluctuations of their bodies, from the obvious to the subtle, as weight comes and goes, muscles contract and extend, energy rises and falls, emotions assert and retreat, and memories emerge and recede, all spilling into movement sequences. Both the gross motor awareness of kinesthesia and the less conscious sensory feedback mechanism of proprioception form the basis of the physical dialogue which is so pivotal to creating the dance. To

A necessity for mutual listening to every kinesthetic shift: Dirk Spruck (*top*) and Roy Wood.

partially listen stifles the dance; to not listen at all impedes the dance altogether. A dance of poor listening may manifest as a series of unintended bumps, uncontrolled slips, both bodies repeatedly breaking contact and restoring it with difficulty. Such dances can frustrate the dancers and limit the direction and quality of the dance. By contrast, being receptive to the many subtle moment-to-moment relays allows the dance its fullest potential and moves it to a substantive exchange in the realm of delight and surprise. The dance may appear lyrical, easily changing heights, shifting speeds, bodies giving the appearance of minimal effort needed to bridge positions. The body can relax into the momentum of the dance and more readily acclimate to the onslaught of activity of which it is part. I welcome dances with keen listeners who tend to point out my habitual responses and offer awareness and the potential for a new movement pattern. Such dances may slow me down as the new awareness presents itself. Or they may assume a faster pace and a new momentum. Either way leaves me awed by the terrain previously unseen and my new navigational skills.

Remaining present and listening go hand in hand. The Contacter behaves as both witness of her own experience and active participant. At any moment, the body bustles with activity: enzymes and hormones release, cells divide, tissues oxygenate, muscles extend, breath circulates, memories surface, and thoughts slip in and out of the foreground. These occurrences may shimmy into and out of awareness or arrive with a queasy thud. As if this flurry of voluntary and involuntary activity isn't enough, the commotion doubles, with one dancer extending awareness to the partner. True, much of the activity never shows up on the radar screen, but one noticeable blip, be it a retraction of an arm or bite of the lip, suffices in urging the dance along.

Attending to the obvious and subtle cues provides the much needed information to determine if a partner is new to the form or preoccupied with thinking, is willing to go into uncharted territory or will greet every invitation to move with resistance. Without trying to design the dance into something pretty, startling, witty, or any other quality, the dancers are guided moment to moment by the many and varied blips, in essence, the inherent energy changes of their separate and adjoining bodies. That energy may be sluggish and heavy or bright and quick. Ideally, one neither judges as good or bad nor translates that energy conceptually, to define it, for instance, as melancholy or graceful or hungry for lunch, and then follow up with a habitual response; rather one stays tuned on the level of animal watchfulness and reactivity, letting the dance evolve out of an instinctive, primordial and preverbal state, which encourages the uncovering of new options.

SAFEGUARDING AGAINST INJURY

Bruising and straining are inevitable with any type of vigorous activity, but such mishaps, even fractures and breaks, are easily avoidable, even in falling, which is an allowable, sometimes sought after thrill. I've participated in and observed numerous dances that push the edges of safety, balance and chaos in a playful yet unsettling battle. Rarely does the first aid kit come out though; when it does, it's usually for splinters or rubbing arnica on a sore muscle.

Aside from easy precautions like emptying pockets of hard, sharp objects, wearing no jewelry, keeping nails trim, and tying back long hair, other practices require vigilance to the body's fluctuations. To avoid injury and allow the body to perform adeptly, Contacters learn to ground and center their weight. Though not exclusive to CI, these principles deal with finding optimal bodily alignment and function, muscles working efficiently, with no system inhibited, no part of the body bearing undue stress. Imagine a root system, firm yet pliant, arising from the floor, extending up through the body. The feet are wide, each toe splayed. Legs are straight, but knees do not lock. The spine elongates, the chest opens, shoulders hang easily from the clavicle, not hiking upward out of customary stress. The head balances on the neck, neither tense nor loose. The gaze softly fixes forward, although the eyes maintain peripheral vision. Like a stem drawing up to the sun from roots deep in the soil, a stem that bends from the wind or a bird's landing, the centered and grounded body yields when necessary. A bent stem recovers its previous position when the bird takes off; the body similarly widens its base before snapping back into a narrower axis. Dancers aim for this flexibility, their balance and strength continually challenged.

THE IMPORTANCE OF CENTERING

This axis, or line of balance, is not a static position. Though a posture to return to repeatedly, it is also a position from which to veer away. Stepping away from the central vein of strength allows play and ventures into territory that can generate the momentum and impetus of falls, flights, spirals, and rolls. Here learning occurs. Here the unknown rushes in, demanding the body focus sharply and awaken instinctive responses. Here, too, arises the potential for harm. If fear sets in, causing muscles to tighten and compromising receptivity, the body may be blocked from tapping into a response that saves the dancer from injury. Centeredness means maintaining a relaxed yet ready state, prepared to meet and, when need be, recover readily from unpredictable, risky moves. Always, however, responsibility rests with individual dancers who must take into account their own skill levels and decide what degree of risk or safety feels welcome.

An ideal body works harmoniously, not antagonistically, each segment of skeleton supported by surrounding bone and tissue. Breath travels easily through the body, suffering no obstruction. The body remains soft yet firm, supple yet strong. The floor offers dynamic support. Explains CI teacher Martin Keogh, "A strong center is fluid and responsive, not rigid. It can hold its ground, resist, and overcome but knows where its edges are. It is content, without the need to go out and find justification for itself.... A strong center is stable, rooted, it can take a position of responsibility, be predictable, face life squarely, be firm in its footing."[5]

Consider this stance home. Consider this the wellspring of all movement.

When I am grounded and centered, my entire body tingles like sunlight glimmering on the ocean surface. I feel deliciously invigorated. Energy and effort come as easily as rest. Intention is not forced but wells up seemingly of its own accord. Support comes from all directions, from flesh and floor, light and whim. Synergy and integration, not struggle, characterize my being and relationship with my partner. Movements flow organically, with only my occasional guidance. I alternate between roles of witness and participant, my experience overlapping my partner's without eclipsing the other's view or controlling the fate of the dance. No one dictates. The dance takes a course of its own, independent of either one of us. We are both willing accomplices in something larger than the two of us. The dance emerges naturally, rising forth from our invisible chemistry. Give finds take, pressure meets resistance, lift follows fall. Perhaps the dance stays low to the floor, and we roll repeatedly across the other's back. Every minuscule shift in

Solid grounding: Rob Smith and Cheryl Pallant.

muscles and every tension and release of tension feels epic. Or the dance adventures into tugs with linked elbows, a series of hops, my partner using my arm to leverage up onto my shoulder where he perches before slipping down my back.

Martial artists rely on grounding and centeredness in keeping their opponents from gaining an advantage. They recommend that feet, shoulder width apart, remain firmly connected to the floor. This position affords great strength and support. Yet CI often finds a partner off the floor altogether, balancing on a shoulder or wrapped around the waist, the feet temporarily relieved of their duty. Feet off the floor excuses no one from the laws of gravity, however. A Contacter still needs to apply centering principles and must find gravity's pull by extending her center into her partner's, the two working together as a single stem which sprouts branches.

CI involves risky maneuvers and lightning quick changes and can put a partner in harm's way. Because of hurling weight and many vulnerable positions, it is easy to topple over, overstress a muscle, or compromise a bone's integrity. Being centered and grounded balances control with letting go, ease with exertion, pliancy with firmness. Attention does not fixate, but widens its focus, a roving and alert eye. It allows the body to tap into its innate wisdom and responsively deal with the unpredictable moving mass of another's body, avoiding excessive stress and potential injury. It reacts when circumstances call for action, calibrating and recalibrating to a dynamically moving environment.

AN INVITATION TO TRESPASS

Given that CI is improvisory, what prevents the dance from becoming anarchy or a free-for-all? Consider, in particular, the fact that the dance already violates social conventions by literally placing two people in each other's personal space, sometimes adjacent, sometimes stacked on top of each other like rambunctious puppies. At many of the larger jams, partners may not even exchange names before sidling up to another's body, the space usually reserved for intimates. What is to prevent dancers from overstepping other boundaries? Well, nothing clears a dance floor faster than a reckless dancer. A partner hell-bent on fulfilling his own agenda with no concern for dialog sends others scurrying in the opposite direction. No one welcomes a dance that appears destined for a physical wreck. Though no waivers get signed beforehand, dancers implicitly agree to engage in a relationship of mutual trust, support, and responsibility, aware that everyone's well-being is at stake. Careful listening assures that partners may approach boundaries, may even step over them, but only through mutual agreement, through unspoken bodily signals.

CI movements are interdependent. Every weight shift, movement, and psychological state directly impacts a partner. Sometimes, for instance, one finds standing possible *only* if the partner offers a stable surface. Or the physical strength and flexibility of one permits the partner to move in ways previously untried. Partners consistently work together, leaning into each other, stepping toward, rolling over, lifting

Left: A high-speed aerial dance: Joe Tranquillo (*falling*) and Dirk Spruck; Mary O'Dwyer and Michael Beckert (*left*). *Right*: A moment later: Dirk Spruck and Joe Tranquillo; Roy Wood and Michael Beckert (background).

up, pressing into, sliding against, giving and taking weight. Separate bodies share motion, space, sweat, a fumble, disorientation, the twist of clothing temporarily pinned by a back or leg. Lives, for the duration of the dance, intimately twine. Such close interrelatedness means that one dancer's responsibility extends to the partner, but not like a parent looking after a child where the parent is the primary caregiver, the child largely oblivious to the protection rendered. Within the dance, responsibility lies primarily with oneself. If a dancer treads into risky material, it is her, not her partner's, responsibility to ensure a safe recovery. Not to say that the partner keeps a hands-off approach, watching indifferently as her unfortunate body crashes to the floor. With movements so closely linked, responsibility for self includes the partner; however, compromising oneself for the sake of another may multiply the potential for harm, not reduce it.

That said, dancers do constantly offer support to one another. Support may manifest as providing the wide plane of a back upon which to roll or stretching out an arm to guide or slow a slide to the

Giving full weight and support: Jessica Wright and Heather Shrock.

40

floor. Assistance may be as simple as extending a leg or making available safe, unwavering shoulders for a 360-degree flight. Dancers learn through trials when support is excessive and turns into unhelpful control and when giving up responsibility frees the dance. For instance, grabbing may feel secure for the grabber, letting her know how and where her partner is moving at all times. But grabbing also restricts free motion, limits the otherwise open-ended direction of the dance, and in some instances, forces the body into an unwelcome trajectory or an unnatural bend.

Frequently testing safety and crossing boundaries, Contacters must establish physical trust. Will my partner counter my weight with her own? If I am hoisted up, will she know what to do and be competent enough to deal with surprises? Will my partner listen attentively enough to not push into areas where I prefer not to go because of my weariness, lack of skill, or fear? These and others issues are addressed nonverbally through the physical information conveyed through physical contact, information that is especially important with new partners

Extending support: Eric Ortega (*bottom*) and Courtney Cooke.

whose movement patterns and ability are as yet unknown. Unspoken agreements about trust and respecting boundaries exist, but what is too risky and off-limits to one dancer may be precisely the material another embraces. Stepping into new territory may feel harmless with one partner, but not another. Discerning differences and determining appropriateness comes back to tuning in to individual bodies, taking each encounter on its own terms, and not applying generalities that may suit one but not the many. A conversation that appeals to one may hold little interest to the next person. Similarly, the ability of one 5'10" dancer may share no correlation with another the same size. One must be alert to projecting assumptions, be they based on size, strength, desire, reputation, or past experience, all of which may be incongruous with the current reality.

MAPPING THE WILDERNESS

Although a challenge of the dance, this need to tune in to the nuances of our partner — and ourselves as well — distinguishes CI. We not only discover what is possible with our partner, but also uncover possibilities we may not have known existed within ourselves. The dance serves as a wilderness for adventure, a playground with its gates unlocked, a laboratory for understanding the functions and physics of the body, a telescope for viewing the mind, a performance staging a relationship.

What makes a dance complete is very much up to each dancer. A dance may contain no rolls whatsoever or never rise more than a few inches up from the floor. The tempo may remain consistent or jerk between two seemingly incompatible extremes. The dance is not about the mastery of particular skills, how frequently one flies, or how smoothly one movement evolves from its predecessor, although for some dancers, these very qualities may determine the worth of the dance. The dance is not valued based on the number or volume of wows or other accolades generated by observers. A Contacter does not receive a different color belt or T-shirt celebrating increased levels of proficiency. The worth of CI is highly individualized, determined by the particular needs of the dancers and how they connect physically and psychically. Addressing a bias she's witnessed among dancers, veteran Contacter Lisa Nelson observes that physical proficiency sometimes obscures other qualities of the dance, like its ability to communicate or stumble into the realm of novelty and surprise. She stresses, "In the people who have been practicing it a long time, I've seen how the refinement of their skills tends toward the mastery of the physical laws, and there's less nuance in the human interaction, where anything can happen."[6] Her comment raises questions about the intent of the dancers. Does the dance reach a height of enjoyment only when dancers master rolls and twists and can prove themselves as adept? When is ease with the dance a disadvantage to the spontaneous impulse and the stumbles into new material? Is one approach to CI better than another?

All teachers and practitioners, depending on background, interests, and culture, color the dance with their own reservoir of experiences. Though a contact point commonly appears in every dance, Contacters may, over time, develop a specific style. An individual Contacter or regional group may stand out, for instance, as more theatrical or physically robust than others. Although there is a body of skills from which to draw, the dance, at its core, derives from improvising and touch. With improvisation as its foundation, the dance is hard to homogenize. Admits a much relieved Curt Siddall, one of the original dancers of CI, "Fortunately there is still no dogma, no rule, the true Contact style. Contact is just us ... expanding on a common experience."[7]

What the dance requires is a body willing to enter the studio and engage with a partner. What it takes is a body eager to come to know the worn kinetic paths as well as the ones less carefully marked. What it takes is a body ready to ride the waves of Being, in stretch, sweat, bend, and press, in balance and at its edge, resisting the supple yet irrefutable laws governing the universe and surrendering now and again to those very same principles as they appear in the dance. What it takes is a body ready to extend beyond the usual reach of its skin.

QUESTIONS

- At what point do you stop trusting the momentum of the dance? When is it a matter of skill, yours or your partner's, and when a matter of size? Is trust based on actual experience or an idea?

- Which part(s) of your body do you favor over others to make contact? Why?

- Do you always dance with the same speed and rhythm? What happens when you rev it up or slow it down?

- How deep or shallow is your breath while dancing? What happens when you invite breath into your belly or the edge of your limbs?

- What is it like to initiate a dance? To decline an invitation? Whichever you do more frequently, try its opposite. Allow accidental collisions, deliberate choices, subtle suggestions, overt no's and yes's.

EXERCISES

Making Contact

Gently sidle up against a partner and find a point of contact. Any part of the body works: arm to arm, back to head. Don't think about it; just go for any available area. Offer a minimum of weight, enough so that you could, if needed, identify through touch the area of the body. Glide across the surface like a sailboat across calm water. Drift horizontally, vertically, and diagonally across your partner. Roll with the body's contours into fleshy and bony areas. Go slow enough to distinguish soft, resilient areas from hard, unforgiving ones, twisting T-shirts from buttons. Play with going faster and slower, high and low on the body, to the floor and back up to standing.

Bit by bit, pour more of your weight into your partner. Lean in, keeping yourself sturdy yet pliant. Note your response when your partner does the same. Feel the support provided. Explore how far you can go. Notice changes in breath, temperature, ease, muscle exertion.

Check your breath regularly to ensure it flows easily and you are not holding it.

Move back and forth along the continuum of contact, rolling, spiraling, sliding, applying a firm and light touch as well as everything in between. Seek out areas of support, leverage, receptivity, strength. Reciprocate. Offer your back, pelvis, head, shoulder. Avoid ankles, knees, places where bones protrude and contain a minimum of cushion, or brush against them lightly. Follow the momentum of the dance without directing its course. Let yourself slip, bump, roll, press, spiral, suggest, yield, engaging with the insistence of gravity.

Variation: Each partner assumes a specific type of contact, such as firm, slippery, wiggly, resistant, without informing each other. Change the quality of contact at will.

Passive/Active

One partner assumes the role of passive mover, the other taking the active role. The active partner introduces movement to the passive one who remains still until receiving a stimulus. The active one can use any part of the body, such as hands, head, knee, and ribs to prompt motion. The passive one responds to the motion introduced, receptive to the impetus of the stimulus, letting the force propel the body. Welcome suggestions, insinuations, inclinations, impulses. Let the energy go only as far as skin and muscle, or as deep as synovial fluid or bile.

Let the stimulus take you to the floor, into a twist, or confine it to a specific muscle. Follow your body's responsiveness rather than decide what seems appropriate. Note the difference between a nudge, a thrust, or a graze. Notice shifts in receptivity and resistance. Travel through the room with the motion unwinding until it trails off completely and your body returns to stillness. Switch roles.

Variation: Do the same, but each partner executes their roles without breaking contact.

Variation: Switch roles regularly without telling your partner.

Intentions and Goals

Decide ahead of time what type of dance you want with a partner. For instance, you might select an energetic, a fluid, or a slow dance. Send the message to every part of your body. Visualize the message as a gas or liquid coming into your limbs and filling every cavity. Welcome it without force. Engage with a partner while maintaining your intention. Observe the edge of your assertions, what gets received, what gets met with resistance, how it influences the flow of the dance. Occasionally suspend your intention. Follow the changes.

Have a second dance with the same partner or another partner with no intentions at all. What are the differences? What happens? Is one easier? More familiar? Surprising? Which type of dance do you have more often? How conscious are you of your intentions?

Centered and Off-Centered

Find your center of gravity, the axis of your spine extending both upward and downward. Your stance should be shoulder width apart, chest open, muscles alert yet relaxed, your feet wide upon the floor. Have a partner try to knock you off center. Start with a few gentle pushes and gradually increase the force without getting outwardly aggressive. Have your partner rest his weight on you, maybe sitting on or leaning against you before lifting off. Continually return to your original centered position. Notice when you lose your balance, when you tense, and what shifts during the recuperation of your centeredness.

Move out from the central axis, expanding your kinesphere as necessary. Imagine your skin expanding outward, along with your ability to sense that which usually lies outside your perceptual range. As your partner pushes, find ways to incorporate a stumble, a sway, or a run into the recuperation of your balance. Play with grace and awkwardness and everything in between.

3

The Knowing Body:
Self and Identity

*New organs of perception come into being as a result of
necessity. Therefore, O man, increase your necessity, so that
you may increase your perception.*
— Rumi

Objective information plays an important role in learning about
ourselves and the world. Such a view makes it fairly easy to arrive at
consensus. We can say, look, there's an arm with a brown spot, and
few would disagree. We can readily agree that our bodies are approximately 70 percent water until some study proves otherwise.

Many of us learn about our bodies the same way, through two-
dimensional illustrations and plastic models. Anatomy books devote
entire chapters to specific systems from the skeletal system to the nervous system to the endocrine system. Each page, reveals complex inter-
active systems largely outside our view, unless we've access to certain
equipment. If we were lucky, our schooling moved our two-dimensional
understanding into the third dimension of plastic human replicas
which, like Mr. Potato Head, came with movable parts, the heart, for
instance, snapping out of position to reveal the lungs.

The conclusion we reach about ourselves from this type of information is a mechanistic one. We learn we have a physical body and
that bodily phenomena can be attributed to equally physical biologi-
cal functions. Understanding about ourselves originates from sources
external to our body. Sweating, we learn, is the body's way of cooling

47

itself when its temperature rises; so if we are sweating, we readily assume our body is hot.

The mechanistic point of view frames us as an object, and objects, like Mr. Potato Head, can be viewed, imposed upon, and manipulated. Parts can be removed, replaced, and, if need be, repaired. The appendix can be cut out, the liver swapped, broken bones fixed.

Assumptions following this thinking can lead us away, not toward, self-knowing. To begin with, we grant objects stability. We presume objects like a rock or a folding chair are inert and constant. On first and even second and third glance, their inherent nature appears not to change. Even something like a flower, which goes from bud to bloom to brown, we assign a certain fixity of identity. More radical alterations like trees toppled by a storm startle us with their sudden transformation into debris, a chore, or firewood. Yet all matter, both sentient and insentient, from our cat to the folding chair, continually undergoes molecular changes. It's just that some motion is more visible and active than others.

OBJECTIVE AND SUBJECTIVE SOURCES OF IDENTITY

An event at the onset of my teens reinforced this mechanistic perspective. A state mandated physical exam, a prerequisite for starting high school, led to the diagnosis of my scoliosis. To say that I have a curved spine is merely a physical description: The degree of curvature and the pinch of nerves alter sensation and muscular strength. The explanation suggests that activities which come easily to others might give me difficulty. The medical papers sent to the school nurse labeled me "disabled," a term full of inherent judgments and expectations. Disabled set me apart from my classmates. Disabled implied I was less capable than others, not on par with the norm. Following the doctor's suggestion, the school nurse sent notices each of the four years to my teachers informing them I was to be excused from gym and barred from participating in physical activities. Though overt signs of my deformity were hardly visible, my absence from gym roused curiosity. Explaining my disability repeatedly reinforced my identity as feeble.

The label followed me into college, with one major difference. The registrar was not informed of my status, and when I signed up for a dance class, no one stopped me. The teacher did not prejudice her lessons either toward the awkward or the graced; no one was excluded from her creative exercises into the body. As a result, for the duration of my college career, I consistently enrolled in dance classes. A remarkable thing resulted. As I rolled on the floor or stepped in rhythm with fellow dancers, I questioned my identity as disabled. Up until then, the label pointed out activities I couldn't do and judged my abilities inferior; I was different, physically aberrant, handicapped. Yet I danced actively, anywhere from two to six hours a day, vigorously moving through space — not unlike fellow able students. When necessary, I could balance on one leg and hand. I could roll on the floor and keep a tempo. I could memorize sequences. I could synchronize gestures with fellow dancers.

Evidence mounted that proved me fairly strong and able. My so-called disability did not set me apart from others any more than my painted fingernails or my interest in philosophy did. My back pain did remain an ongoing focus of my attention and inhibited some movements, but I excelled in other ways — again not unlike fellow students with their own unique blend of strengths and weaknesses. My curved spine set me apart from them, but their height or accent similarly distinguished them from me.

Our educational system is biased toward what psychologist and education theorist Howard Gardner refers to as logical-mathematical and linguistic intelligences, a type of learning which emphasizes science and reason.[1] Understanding comes about through objectifying a subject, depersonalizing it, setting it outside our body. What becomes worthy of attention and study are common, measurable experiences, not anything that is subjective, idiosyncratic, sensate, ephemeral, or numenous. At fault is not the classes per se, but how they're taught and the perspectives omitted. Primary and secondary school students rarely if ever go on field trips to archeological sites to dig through dirt;

instead they look at pictures accompanying a book's narrative. A senior can graduate at the top of the class without ever having played a musical instrument. He will likely learn that sound is vibration detectable by the hearing organs, but he will miss out on figuring out how to wrap his lips around the horn's mouthpiece to generate not just a haphazard blast of sound, but music.

Schools emphasize memorization of facts and opinions while neglecting experiential, heuristic methods. Visual and performing arts classes, which rely upon hands-on, experiential learning, are often the first to fall under the budgetary axe. In many school districts, no class time at all is devoted to developing overlooked intelligences, which Gardner categorizes as musical, bodily-kinesthetic, spatial, interpersonal, intrapersonal, and naturalist. Individual discovery and engagement is often the tolerable but not encouraged stepchild of the dominant, more objective methodologies.

OVERCOMING LONG-HELD BELIEFS

An external perspective permeates popular culture, where bodies are commonly and vaingloriously objectified. Magazines with seductive covers crowd aisles at grocery checkout counters, and flashy television images transmit messages about who we ought to be. Repeatedly we are shown the "ideal" body, slim and toned, a body that may have come as a result of a near starvation diet and services like liposuction, botox, or airbrushing. Such glorified bodies frequently come with alluring smiles, sexually provocative gazes, and glimpses of flesh, tempting viewers into a way of thinking and, in many cases, purchasing a product. The reflection in our mirror at home pales in comparison to the perfected image celebrated by the media.

The message spread by various media is compelling and instigates a chain of events. Pointing out our cellulite, excess curves, or any other unsightly shortcoming, media then tries to make sure we don't despair: it prescribes treatment. Innumerable magazine articles, books, and videos describe how to achieve so-called milestones like slim thighs, six-pack abs, blemish-free skin, pearly white teeth. Just subscribe to the idea, the exercise, and buy the corresponding brand. The treatments promise to transform us into attractive, happy individuals — a causally flawed logic. Consciously or not, inundated with such messages and yearning for approval, many of us buy into these ideals, believing their truths, conditioned since grade school to heed external messages. We have fewer experiences, in comparison, that reinforce building strength and confidence from within and learning to be satisfied with who we are, to discover and celebrate our natural shape and unique character. A skewed self-appreciation and, in many cases, outright self-denigration results from receiving one type of message without balancing it with another.

As a result, we go to the gym to work out and criticize those extra five pounds. We try to control our body as much as possible, hostile toward the givens of our birth. Even if we are successful in achieving the ideal body, we may still feel confounded when our newly altered body fails to make us feel significantly happier than when we started.

Mass media's obsession with thinness has contributed to a cult of anorexia where eating disorders and body-image distortions have become the norm. More than half of my female college students diet constantly, believing they are overweight. It doesn't matter if they weigh 105 or 150 pounds at a height of 5'6". Self-criticism about their bodies is as common as talk about the weather. The belief shows up in their dancing; to avoid letting their partner learn to what degree they're overweight, only reluctantly do they lean into their partner, dodging that ever-important physical connection that allows the dance to unfold. The contact remains tentative, a game of withdraw and hide. The dance, no more than half-hearted grazes, shies away or altogether avoids the bloom of its potential. I've read numerous student journals from both dance majors and non-majors who admit to disdain for their bodies. They want to control their bodies, to impose ideas upon them, but they are ill-equipped or unwilling to get to know them. They don't see the chasm between their preconceived notions and the flesh of reality.

CI becomes the very vehicle for change. Exercises like leaning into partners or rolling across a back prompt a confrontation with their attitudes and prejudgments. In the process, they learn they're not as fat or weak or unacceptable as they first thought. They also discover the correlation between attitude and ability; new and challenging movements are more easily learned when the mind cooperates with the body and is not issuing denigrating decrees with every stretch and bend.

Media isn't the only external source of information. Organized religion offers its theological worldview and how to behave within it. Similarly the legal system tells us which behaviors are lawful and which illegal. Society, family, colleagues and peers all provide models and guidelines for appropriate behavior for each gender and age group. Be it eating, achieving professional success, shopping, playing sports, or interacting at parties, we learn which behaviors are permissible along with their proper protocols. Again, the messages imposed upon us come from sources outside our immediate, lived, sensate experience. Learning does not arise out of subjective experience, from attentiveness and perceptual refinement, from sensing the tension or laxity of our muscles or the bruising of skin against bone. Conclusions and beliefs are not a result of personally earned experiences, but ones that are borrowed or transferred. Such appropriation is helpful and necessary at times. Much learning occurs through observing and adopting. But it can be harmful when we entertain no options, have no maps for getting there, believe no alternatives exist or don't know how to combine perspectives.

This appropriating point of view has its place and its abuses. Trouble comes when we rely on it as our primary way of knowing and devalue or outright ignore other perspectives. Trouble comes when we don't recognize to what extent its tentacles have wrapped themselves around our engagement with the world, strangling perceptions, behavior, and expectations. Trouble comes when we forget that concepts and seemingly fixed ideas aren't as solid as they appear. Trouble comes when we accept ideas prescribed for us without question. Trouble comes when we readily favor another's view over personal experience, inadvertently neglecting the potent seeds and fertile soil of individual engagement.

Exclusively subscribing to the dominant view leaves out heuristic methods, where learning takes place not through external sources telling us what's so and imposing preconceived rules, ideals, and constructs upon us, but through personal sensate interaction with the world. Wholesale endorsement of objectivity ignores the importance of individual differences and events or qualities not readily explicable. We may end up neglecting experiences and impressions dwelling in the hinterlands, a puzzling vision, a melodic refrain, a twitch, all of which can cue us, to details of our personal embodiment. Depending on how deeply invested we are, fear, comfort, or habit may dictate perception, blocking any route to alternatives. Unless, that is, fate sticks out its foot upon which we stumble. Unless misfortune compels us to look more closely at circumstances. Unless a benign guide points to an activity that challenges those habits. Unless that activity leads to questions arising not only from intellect alone but also direct, lived experience.

Dance teaches the difference between ideas and reality. New dancers learn there is frequently a gap between their idea about what a movement looks like and the procedure involved in carrying it out. Between the two exists myriad obstacles, few insurmountable. After

Known and unknown selves: Richmond jammers.

failing repeatedly to fully extend an arm overhead, the elbow unable to straighten, we may learn that a weak muscle needs strengthening or the ligaments around the scapula are too tight. A belief like seeing oneself as too fragile may impede the very activity that helps develop shoulder muscles. Or the belief may restrict the breath necessary to lifting the arm. Navigating and discovering the personal terrain of our body is imperative if we're ever going to come close to knowing who we are and the abilities that may be dormant in us.

REDEFINING THE SELF

CI reveals the body as a process, not a static, passive entity awaiting definition. The dance demonstrates the importance of personal engagement with a world that is constantly changing. Assisting in the development of perceptual skills, specifically kinesthetic, kinetic, tactile, and proprioceptive ones, CI encourages a body to embody itself, to notice the many sensory impressions passing through the filter of skin — the sweat dripping on our neck, the glimmer at the window, the tingle in our toe, the compression of our ribs, the discomfort from last night's dream that won't fade with the light.

Attention concentrates our focus. The act of looking, or sensing, brings into focus what we are perceiving. The very act of perceiving influences the object of our perception. For instance, stretching my legs in front of me while I sit on the floor seems like a simple enough position, yet once I concentrate on the extension of each leg, I notice many minute actions, each with repercussions. I find that there's a difference between pointing my feet toward the ceiling or pointing them forward; a difference between lengthening my spine or letting it sag; a difference between breathing from my belly or from my lungs; a difference between setting my gaze a few inches or several feet away. The matter complicates further when I try to raise one leg while leaving the other flat. How and where I place attention alters the way I execute the movement. I may be told what is so about these movements, but that conclusion may change once I examine it by experiencing it myself.

54

This phenomenological perspective, which breaks down motion into discrete steps, emphasizes the active role the body takes in perceiving itself in relation to the world. The relationship is not one-sided, but a reflexive, two-way street with consciousness as a meeting place between dynamic entities. The world imposes itself upon us, knocking or banging on the door, while similarly we impose ourselves upon the world. States philosopher Maurice Merleau-Ponty about what he sees as the body's paradox, "[M]y body simultaneously sees and is seen.... It sees itself seeing; it touches itself touching; it is visible and sensitive for itself. It is not a self through transparence, like thought, which only thinks its objects by assimilating it, by constituting it, by transforming it into thought.... Visible and mobile, my body is a thing among things; it is caught in the fabric of the world."[2]

In CI, weight presses upon us and we press back, countering it with support. We meet the gaze of our partner and perhaps turn away. We stay in rhythm with our partner, discover harmony, or introduce a new tempo. Both bodies influence the movements of each other. I

Strength meets strength: Brandon Crouder and Kenika Kiante Canty.

am the central object in which the world of others revolve, an infinite number of people and objects imposing their worlds upon me. I am also one among numerous subjects imposing ourselves upon others. Continually my senses receive and perceive others, my skin, ears, and other senses mingling with and influencing all they encounter. Dance writer Ann Cooper Albright summarizes similarly, "I am not a self housed in a predominantly passive body. Rather, my body and my self are continually creating and being created by the world around me. This dialectical relationship of self and world can provide an important model for any discussion about the body's role in organizing reality."[3]

The body is not a blank screen, a tabula rasa, receiving whatever gets projected upon it, although the mechanistic perspective may lead to this conclusion. Nor is the body separate and isolated, the sole creator of its world and the world around it. Rather, senses open doors to both a private, internalized realm, and a public, external one, the skin between worlds permeable and porous. Senses awaken in the announcement of stimuli as innumerable nerve pathways crank into motion. The present moment unfolds its palpable riches, revealing not only a readily perceivable side but also glimpses of a less visible underbelly.

Australian Contacter Helene Gronda refers to the attentiveness found in CI as "practicing the body." Mind is not the director, but a supporter, in partnership with the body. Likening CI to other body practices such as Alexander Technique or yoga, she explains, "It is the ability to follow a somatic process using heightened internal perception. It combines an embodied consciousness and a research attitude.... It is a choice for engagement with the body rather than its mastery, but without negating or punishing the desire for control."[4]

Every moment of CI shows to what degree conspicuous and subtle changes are guaranteed. As the dancing body exerts and orients itself in space, pressed against the irrefutable reality of another body, the motion and mass of the bodies alert the senses. With a foot flying toward the face or shoulder skin stretching, circumstances change rapidly, and many responses cannot be anticipated or deliberated. The senses cannot afford to be lackadaisical. Be it a gentle or demanding dance, the presence of fellow moving bodies compels the senses to pay sharp attention, to discern every shift in weight, however subtle, and to act accordingly. A predilection for safety, avoiding broken bones and such, requires the body make instant decisions. There are numerous times when I find myself in a novel position with my partner and the quick pace of the dance doesn't permit an analysis of the situation. Instead I trust that my body knows what to do. Once I was lying atop my partner back to back, feet off the floor, my limbs interlaced with his. As our weight shifted, mine prompted a quick somersault over his head, lowering us both to the floor where we tumbled repeatedly, entwined the whole way, a movement series that previously I had not imagined possible, or not without injury.

Whether we resist, yield, fold to the floor, or extend our backs reveals how we negotiate our mass, space, and relationships. Our movements may be out of character, a spiciness provoked by the moment, or may clue us to familiar patterns replicated as often on the floor as off. Valuable feedback comes through our partners' responses to our movements, through the causal relationship of interacting bodies, and

Reinforcing strength with support: Steven Harris and Patty Pickering.

the emergence of sensory reactions, the sweat and flush, awkwardness and ease, reluctance and willingness. The supportive and trusting attitude of CI encourages acknowledging our impulses and tendencies, confirming who we are in the very moment of becoming, a simple act with profound consequences.

In paying attention to what presents itself— the sounds, images, ideas and memories — we get to see our raw as well as hard-crusted contents prior to censure, distraction, or bias. Borrowing techniques from CI, movement therapist Sondra Fraleigh developed a method she calls Contact Unwinding which she uses for healing. Explaining her method, she says, "The relationship is one where the therapist is listening to the patterns that emerge and following them as the partners move together." Once flow is established, the therapist "can then guide the participant toward new options in their movement pattern."[5]

A TOUCH ISSUE

A prime example of a belief colliding with experience is the hurdle many Contacters overcome in determining what degree of touch is appropriate. Standard social conduct is explicit in its guidelines. Limited touch is permissible between parents and children, the details of propriety changing with the age of the children. Lovers indulge in a wider range of touch — in private. Casual touch is forbidden between strangers. One does not usually rest a hand, even briefly, on a stranger at a café. We apologize for any accidental knock or graze against another at the counter or in line. Strangers on crowded elevators avoid any sort of acknowledgment, briefly disembodying. One's entire being withdraws, arms tuck, and eyes fix on the illuminating numbers awaiting the chosen floor. Though, we are very close, we pretend not to notice the lemon scent of shampoo, the softness of the cashmere sweater brushing an arm, or any other detail that comes with close proximity.

In CI, there is no eighteen inches of safety between individuals. Distance between partners disappears altogether. Many new Contacters commonly hesitate and inhibit themselves. They can't readily dismiss societal messages to keep a safe distance. They tread apprehensively into previously forbidden territory, navigating unfamiliar boundaries of propriety while society's strictures grip at their attempt to feel at ease in the dance, to allow breath and movement their fullest potential. Commonly, initial dances may involve little more than superficial brushes against each other. Whatever contact occurs is often dominated by areas of familiarity and common acceptability like hands or arms. If torsos or necks meet, they do so briefly, sometimes with laughter and a blush. But once subsequent dances incite neither disapproval nor wrath, partners are encouraged to extend the touch and offer more weight.

Inevitably questions and discomfort arise concerning sensuality, which CI elicits, and sex, which draws attention away from the often demanding and risky moves of the dance. Paxton warns against getting involved in the "gland game," a distraction which can lead to injury.[6] CI is tactile in its exchanges, sensuous as well, but this is dance, not a date, and even a thrilling dance of mutual strength, risk, and ability is not prelude to a courtship off the floor. The dance is no more a courtship than is wrestling or rugby. Often the intense athletic demands of the dance shove any preoccupation with sex aside, attention necessarily riveted to physical safety. Thinking about sex while dancing suggests a fixed focus which neglects the wider spectrum of the dance as it continually evolves from one sensation to the next. Those who attend jams with exclusive intentions of finding a sexual partner are typically unwelcome.

Sexual attraction may occur, as it can in any circumstance. However, the dance generates a bounty of sensory experiences, of which sexual feeling is only one. The dance demonstrates that touch serves a role beyond sex, a conclusion that one with repressed sexual attitudes may find unfathomable. Moreover, the intention of CI is not to size up a partner for romance or sex, but to develop physical skills and widen attention, playing and conversing nonverbally, exploring movement, and coming home to our bodies. It asks that we join consciousness with bodily awareness and not quarantine them in separate boxes. It asks us to abandon Cartesian duality and invite a more fully embodied participation in the inherent harmony of our bodies' intelligence.

It encourages the emergence of a self that germinates like a latent seed into bloom. It dares us to partake in an evolutionary dance with trillions of cells. The dance articulates a marvelous yet rigorous journey into sparsely inhabited regions that fall nothing short of our glorious humanity. And we do so in solidarity with a partner whose motion, weight, press, play, and touch continually root us in our physical presence.

Establishing an awareness contrary to cultural conditioning, neutralizing the message that claims all touch is sexual, and discovering touch's wider applicability require effort. Widespread repressive attitudes towards sex lead to imposed silences, confusion, misunderstanding, and dark ghettos of thought. Instead of celebrating the body and reaping its benefits, we are often encouraged to denigrate it, to reside elsewhere, at an address that makes little reference to skin, blood, breath or desire. Instead of developing tools for accepting the global dimensions of who we are, we are tricked repeatedly into restricted views or into looking away entirely.

UNRAVELING TRUTH

Feeling at ease with one's body and establishing a genuine point of view, which may run contrary to popular ideas, means butting heads with a barrage of convincing messages from parents, media, and society that suggest otherwise. It means valuing personal experience and challenging the status quo by learning to read our own cues. It means unraveling the threads that keep us clothed in a certain perspective. It means following our own somatic journey, the dangling threads and impulses which may include contradictory, difficult, threatening, and idiosyncratic signals, a process which contributes to learning through firsthand experience. The task rarely comes easily since many of us are ill-educated and ill-equipped to trust our own experience, illiterate in reading the body. One try alone does not suffice in stripping away cultural robes. Dorothy had to overcome numerous obstacles and needed a trio of supporters before conjuring the gumption to pull back the curtain of Oz.

Confronting self while confronting another: Cathy Magill (*bottom*) and Beth Parsons.

Welcoming such an opportunity, Ron Estes took up CI after encountering a group of men who astonished him with their physical ease with each other. "What they had in common was they did Contact. I said, I want that. I want to be able to have an experience of being a kid again, to have a presence with men and women where sex isn't an issue.... We're simply dancing. I find that very liberating."[7] Says Breanna Rowland in her class journal, "Now I remember why I used to love to dance. Before all the competition and eating disorders. It was about freedom. It was the ability to make the whole world go away for a period of time and still be doing something constructive.... It was about fear but also respect. A way to be proud of who you are."[8]

Highlighting differences between personal and appropriated reality, CI focuses attention on phenomenal interaction to such a degree that it becomes difficult to ignore our physical responses, reflexivity, and accompanying insights. It is hard to ignore a sweating body or the heart's pounding as breath rushes in and out of the lungs. This awareness may not, however, make it any easier to accept or integrate into our culturally defined worldview, an experience not limited to Americans. Experienced in classical Indian dance, martial arts, and yoga, Calcutta-based Contacter Ranjabati Sircar encountered dancers struggling with this very issue.

> Although touch is part of classical dance, it has always been for a very specific reason and for a limited time, in a clearly demarcated manner.... I found dancers perfectly able to touch one another in a way that expressed "humanness," but completely foxed at the prospect of exploring touch as a part of technique. In other words, they were comfortable touching another to express emotions in a pedestrian way, but were not comfortable when asked to explore it as a dynamic it itself, related to movement and weight.[9]

It's inevitable that Contacters encounter societal beliefs and practices in sharing intimate space with another. Who that other is influences the dance and reveals adopted biases not only toward touch, but also toward gender, religion, race, and nationality. Because CI poses no restrictions on who dances with whom and regards all partners as equals, it's not only possible that a man dances with woman, but also a man with a man, a woman with a woman, a straight person with a gay one, a Unitarian with a Libertarian, a Muslim with a Jew. Depending on our cultural, religious, and sexual orientation, some of these combinations may be more charged than others. Some Contacters may avoid the confrontation altogether; others grab hold of the opportunity to trek across social and cultural boundaries, watching and learning through the thoughts and feelings surfacing in the process.

The dance raises questions about culturally favored behaviors and the actions and attitudes we may downplay in our attempt to fit into society. For instance, American culture values physical strength and assertiveness in men. Subsequently, many men devote time to developing these abilities and receive societal accolades for doing so. These traits appear in the dance in men's proclivity toward frequently lifting women or men with slight builds, even though no rule says a CI dance is incomplete without it. A woman with sufficient training can lift a man regardless of his size, yet she may inhibit her physical strength and assertiveness because our culture values delicacy and deference over more muscled displays. The question worth asking is whether the lifts or any other movements evolve naturally from the contours of the dance or from gender expectation.

Contacter Gloria Lee caught herself in the clutch of social conditioning. On first learning the dance, she was particularly apprehensive about men who she assumed couldn't be sensitive enough to respect her diminutive frame. After her first weekend jam, she quickly learned otherwise. "The men were so gentle. I usually don't think of men that way."[10] The experience offered Lee new information to adjust her understanding.

CI shows no favoritism toward masculine or feminine behaviors and doesn't assign either sex a given role in the dance. Individual ability and the whims arising in the moment determine the direction and content of the dance. Gentle glides across a cotton-clad back, a furious tussle, weight nudging a stretch or gasp, undulating hips — none of these movements are exclusive to women or to men. Relishing the androgyny of the dance, Contacter Richard Aviles explains, "I can be all of what I am in Contact. If you want to use the binary of masculine and feminine qualities, it's all there.... Expectations and social scripts of what it's like to be masculine are out the window. I don't have to follow those narratives anymore."[11]

The dance is an ongoing process of large and small developments: perceptual shifts for some may occur with only a few dances. One twirl around the shoulders or headfirst slide down a back may sufficiently resolve concerns about trust, for instance. For others, shifts, particularly significant ones, may be more gradual. When she was in her early twenties, K, who prefers to remain anonymous, was assaulted by a man who raped her and attempted to take her life. For years, she identified herself as a victim. Then she took up martial arts and CI. In fifteen years, "I went from being a victim to feeling tough and strong as a martial artist, then feeling myself soft and gentle and able to open up through Contact. Different things used to push my buttons. Now, nothing triggers my stuff. It's wonderful fun and such a creative way to play and move."[12]

Sharing space: Sharon Russell, John Swift, Kevin Heffernan, and Brad Stoller.

A SOURCE OF POWER

With every lift and fall, CI tests definitions, comfort levels, pre-conceptions, and boundaries — essentially the stories we believe about ourselves and the world. Be it a compelling interior voice that won't quit or a quality of movement, we find the extent to which ideas inhabit us. Ideas live through us, are us, manifesting as our slouching shoulders, the tilt of our head, the flush in our cheeks, our willingness or reluctance to engage with a partner, the way we stomp or tiptoe through the hours. The need for sensory alertness while dancing forces us out of our heads, away from typical thoughts and familiar narratives, which distance us from felt experience. In the dance, we instead inhabit the entirety of our body, now adrenalized as we mobilize uncommonly through space, rolling like tumbleweed along the floor or vaulting like a released spring against a partner's chest.

If we're catapulting through space while caught in thought, we endanger ourselves and our partner with our inattentiveness to the environment, to skin and bones, balance and counterbalance. Ideas become useless fluff, senseless mechanisms separating body from space and the constantly moving circumstances of dancing bodies. What's needed is our fully awake reflexive faculties, a keen alertness to the ever-changing physical world.

Hands may have to grab, breath deepen, muscles relax or extend deeply into a stretch as an arm or head seeks a surface, or offers one, a horizon or edge on which to situate temporarily. Perhaps we are standing upside down, balanced in a turned, refigured world, a moment of stillness amid seeming chaos. Or perhaps our legs fly up toward the ceiling or down toward the floor with perfect control. Up, down, thigh, neck — usually we don't take the time to define position or what body part touches where.

Surfaces matter. Center matters. Breath matters. Contact matters. Energy matters. Safety in play. Risk with reserve. Two, maybe three or four, dancing as one, a fellowship of selves, the body as an instrument of play.

Relying on kinesthetic intelligence, centeredness, and counterbalance: Veronica Ramon and Cheryl Pallant.

CI boosts blood flow, increases heart rate, oxygenates tissue, increases energy. The body becomes enlivened, flush with systems roused from torpor, from habit, routine, and repetition. The body awakens to itself and the presence of additional bodies in a creatively shared space. Perhaps our partner asks for quiet. Or control. Or whimsy. A casual drift or superficial response in CI is unsatisfying. In a physical exchange, the partnership requires sensitivity and responsibility.

Although they try, Contacters may find they cannot control the wave of the moment any more than they can control waves in an ocean. Dancers learn to ride the twined currents of bodies, the inherent energy that rises and stills, pools and swells. Individual egos combine into a collective body that shuffles shapes and offers constant variations.

CI brings home unignorable sensations for committing investigations into living — if we choose to do so. The dance immerses us in the voluptuous pulsing moment and gives us an opportunity to move creatively through space. The paths of this activity allow for explorations into the overgrown and neglected, the embryonic and the latent, the bewildering and the captivating — landscapes rarely visited, uninhabited spaces not yet discovered or begging for renewal. CI stirs the body from its slumber.

Embodied involvement suggests that sometimes sweat is not only sweat but also a somatic link to our personal body, perhaps leading to a hidden memory or pointing out a blind spot in our actions. It may also imply that there is no meaning other than the heart's thump and the body's need for cooling. As surfaces of body press beyond surfaces, the dance can foster immersion into living rich with symbols, clues, whispers, nudges, and visions.

When the body awakens, the result is savory morsels for a choreographer, painter, engineer, ecologist or anyone who wants to live deeply. Source and resource. Dialog, not lecture. An active, vibrant body welcomes stimuli, knowing when to say yes, and when to say no, when to receive an impetus and when to push an unwanted or oppressive force away. A discerning self moves through its many seasons. Whether we identify ourselves as Son, Mother, Dancer, Student, Frail,

Charming, or Difficult, the dance floor reveals identities as mutable and as varied as the dance.

QUESTIONS

- What are your parents' attitudes about their bodies? How do their ideas manifest? In what ways are your attitudes the same or different? How do any of these attitudes influence your dance?

- In what ways do you keep yourself from dancing more fully? What inhibits you?

- What beliefs do you hold about the appearance and ability of your body? Which beliefs make you proud and which give you shame?

- How do you think others see you as a dancer? How do their views affect your dancing and your risk-taking?

- When does your alertness dull? When do you stop feeling sensation? What prompts your mind to chatter and shift focus away from the contact point to your internal monolog? What prompts you to disconnect from your partner?

- When is an uncomfortable dance exactly what is needed?

- What expectations limit you?

EXERCISES

Altering Ego

With a partner, come up with five words that describe your personality. Then come up with words that are unlike you. Aim for an identity that is your polar opposite. Once you have a clear idea about this supposed person, do the same with your partner. Discuss the ways this person might behave in various scenarios and how this person might walk and stand. As if putting on a costume, wear this person's body. Dance as these Not-Yous, beginning with a solo dance and then making contact.

Gendering

Make two groups, one of women, the other men. Make a list of events, activities, and approaches that you consider gender specific. For instance, giving birth, going bald, suffering from PMS. When both groups have completed their lists, one group reads the items listed while the other group demonstrates them through movement. Once an item is read, allow time enough for movements to evolve before going on to the next item on the list. When the group reading completes the list, switch roles.

Appealing

While dancing with a partner, notice qualities or specific movements that appeal to you. Perhaps it's the pivot off a hip or the solidity of your partner. Make a simple comment about what is appealing. For instance, "The press of your hip against my shoulder is appealing." Or "That the dance is remaining on the floor is appealing." Take turns making statements. Keep them brief. Notice the impact of the statements upon the dance, how they may affect its direction. Periodically return to dancing silently.

Telling a Lie

Tell someone a huge lie about yourself as a dancer. Exaggerate. Pretend. Play. Go all out. Go into detail. Let your partner ask questions and get you to make up answers. Notice the physical changes in your body as you fib. In what ways are what you've said true? Attempt to dance with some of the lies.

Reclaiming Innocence

Imagine yourself as a child. Choose an age when you crawl to discover the world. Ambulate on all fours, as low to the floor as feels natural. Cry. Smile in unabashed joy. Find ways to know the floor, your movements, any persons and objects you encounter. Indulge in primal wonderment. Move through each of the senses. Listen viscerally. Feel sound vibrate inside your ear and further into your body. Feel light and shapes upon your eyes and skin.

Progress through the years until you reach your current age. You can rise to your feet and walk around the space or do simple movements in a solo dance, staying close to the floor. Notice when your critical voice begins to speak up. What age are you? What is this voice saying? How does its comments alter how you move? When do the comments and the feelings associated with them eclipse discovery and wonderment?

Try to incorporate a more innocent attitude into your current age. Or return to an age when innocence came easily. Engage in a contact dance. Notice how it differs from your usual dance.

Chance Encounters

As you walk through the woods, drive across town, or get rocked by the subway on your way to the studio that hosts your jam, randomly choose an object along your journey: the cry of an owl, the color on a billboard, the scrape of someone's bag against your leg. In the studio, get to know the object and its resonance with you. Whether it's an object you carry to the jam or had to leave behind, get familiar with its qualities: its depth of color; the sharpness or smoothness of its edges; its heaviness or lightness; its size and texture. Find a way to embody it. Perhaps manifest the object through a series of movements or by imitating its shape in your arm. Carry it into a partnered dance and notice its influence. How hard or easy is it to sustain? When does one of its qualities change? If you are forced to let it go, what precipitates the action?

4
The Entitled Body:
Politics and Privilege

Politics don't disappear but take place inside my body.
— Kathy Acker

In 2000, I traveled to Budapest to attend a gathering of European Contact teachers. For this annual event with a rotating host country, the Hungarian site was chosen to vitalize Hungary's CI community and provide affordable access for Eastern European dancers. Exchanging teaching insights and class lessons, the group, comprised of about 125 teachers from 22 countries (participants from outside Europe were also present), gathered one evening to talk about the state of CI in their respective countries.

The differences were astounding. Rivaling the United States, both Germany and Argentina boasted consistently active jams. Germany sustained jams in a number of cities with sizeable attendance at multi-day events. In Buenos Aires, numerous jams and classes occurred throughout the week. By contrast, Hungary had only several dozen dancers. As dancers from each country reported, disparities often came down to financial support and government policy. For instance, prior to the collapse of communism several years earlier, Hungarians were limited to government sanctioned dances, which meant backing for only ballet and folk dance. Communism prohibited any Western imports, and CI received no special exclusion from the law. Few dancers in Hungary or surrounding countries like Slovakia and Estonia had been exposed to the dance unless they traveled outside the country for school or a festival.

The Russians talked about how, under communism, they danced secretly in basements and other clandestine locations; any public showing of CI could get them arrested. No producing a concert, setting up classes, or posting flyers innocuously on bulletin boards. CI was illegal, tantamount to smuggling, operating in the black market. Practicing CI made one an outlaw, a criminal, an endangerment to the government and its ideology. An American art like CI was strictly forbidden.

With the fall of communism, Russian Contacters came out of hiding, and more and more dancers were taught the form. Approval from bureaucrats did not, however, mean a huge proliferation of new Contacters. Hosting a several day CI event or producing a concert requires money, and as our Hungarian hosts explained, though their government no longer condemned the American import, allocating funds to support it was not among its priorities. Similar sentiments came from a number of local institutions asked to donate facilities or funds for scholarships.

THE LIBERTY TO MOVE

To Westerners with little or no exposure to an overtly oppressive regime, regulations against something as seemingly innocent as CI may seem absurd. Few of us can claim a criminal record or feel legally threatened from dancing (though I was once questioned by the police in New Orleans when my gleeful body danced impromptu in an abandoned warehouse along the Mississippi River). We may well ask what's so dangerous about CI. Where's the political charge? What's so provocative?

I don't mean to downplay the substantial differences between countries, the history of governments, and the impact upon people. Rather, with an eye toward who gets to dance, I want to focus on the similarities between countries, even regimes as divergent as democracies and dictatorships.

Difficulties that prevent many of us from attending a jam are more likely the result of scheduling conflicts, needing to attend work or school or spend time with family. Or perhaps the obstacle is one of transportation; our car is in the shop and there is no available public transport. As we travel to a jam, far from our thoughts is the political privilege of our jamming, the gift fate has delivered — money, time, and opportunity conspiring in favor of our showing up in the studio. Similarly, once on the dance floor, our concerns likely focus on who will dance with us, what sort of dance it may be, or how to avoid injury.

Jam organizers know well the difficulties of pulling together an event, be it a weekly dance or the less frequent multi-day events. Aside from finding a suitable space with a decent wood floor, free of splinters and concrete, most organizers face difficulties in generating financial support for the craft. Although Americans claim the arts are important, their wallets do not follow their words. Funding available to sponsor dance, like all the arts, is meager. Support for dance has diminished in the last few decades. Government funding for the arts in general has experienced serious declines on local, state, and federal levels. Post 9-11, states were hit hard, reducing arts funding by almost half.[1]

One may conclude that neither the government nor private and public institutions consider it a priority. As a result, those who organize jams or produce concerts must find creative ways to subsidize the work and make it affordable to dancers who typically earn little money. There are regulations against the dance, but the opportunities are not nearly as plentiful as, say, race car driving or basketball, both vigorous industries with ample commercial support. And though more and more American universities offer classes in CI, embracing a rich dance history, many more individuals get exposed to it through private classes run by a peripatetic group of teachers who travel from city to city, and country to country, sharing the dance. Attendance fees at these classes remain intentionally low, with work study and scholarships frequently offered, ensuring access to dance regardless of the bulk or leanness of the wallet.

Even if CI were met by widespread institutional support, I don't believe such a specialized dance would ever be embraced by the masses. In a culture with a norm that promotes disembodiment and an outward gaze, the motivation, patience, and self-reflection needed to pursue a somatic process concerned with studied subtleties, not blatant or trendy displays of bravado, is hard to conjure. Although the dance can be both thrilling and meditative, it carries neither the intensely adrenalized allure of bungee jumping nor the easily grasped grace of in-line skating. Additionally, it's hard to reduce CI to a sound bite.

Nonetheless, its limited availability and some of the accompanying obstacles involved lead me to ask who gets to dance and under what circumstances. How much of the privilege to dance is a result of political climate, from policy makers, and how much from other sources? Who determines who can dance and what dances get supported? What role does class, ethnicity, gender, or something as seemingly unpolitical as physiology play in determining who receives encouragement for their movements on the dance floor? One may quickly assume that anyone can dance; all that's needed is time, some cash, and a willing body. However, this simply isn't so.

OPEN DOORS FOR SOME

Not all dancers are treated equally, even in America where constitutional rhetoric guarantees individual liberties for all people. Even in this country with its mystique of realizing dreams, dance doesn't escape exemption from political influence. Dance is not a nondiscriminatory, all-accepting activity available to anyone who wants to slip on his dance shoes, or in the case of CI, remove shoes altogether. Dance is subject to its fair share of regulation.

For instance, ballet, the highly respected and stylized classical form imported from Europe, comes with several highly specific restrictions. Most companies want men and women of a certain size. From a ballet manual addressed to the would-be student, the "ideal reflection" for a woman is described as "a head neither too large nor too small, well-poised on a slim neck; shoulders of some width but with a slope gently downward; small bust, waist, buttocks; a back that is straight but not too rigid; well-formed arms hanging relaxed from the shoulders; delicate hands; slim straight legs with smooth lines in the back and front; a compact foot that arches easily — all of this totaling a slim silhouette of ballet perfections." For men, the required physique is less detailed: "[I]t is generally considered to be strong, and well muscled without excess weight, or bulk, the shoulders wider than the waist and hips, and the height minimum of 5'6"."[2]

Earlier restrictions were more discriminating. Prior to 1850, the stage was considered no place for women, who would have to leave behind their socially esteemed roles as mothers and wives, disgracing themselves and their families by partaking in what was then perceived as the tawdriness of theater. Consequently, all roles were assigned to men. Race restrictions were more severe, a result of segregation policies. If they wanted to dance, African-Americans needed to form their own companies, as Katherine Dunham did in 1931 with Negro Dance Group, which blended African-American rhythms with ballet. When the stage finally grew more accepting of women and people of color, the doors of dance still opened primarily only to those from the upper class, often liberal backgrounds, whose families could afford to send their children to classes or performing arts schools for specialized training.

IN STEP AND OFF

Ballet appeals to traditional Judeo-Christian values. Considered high art, ballet demonstrates incredible body control with codified movements and vocabulary. Primarily geared toward entertainment for the upper class, originally for nobility, classical movements emphasize a heavenward (chaste) direction — hence numerous lifts, leaps, and toes on pointe. The lower body remains rigid, relatively devoid of life — none of the gyration, shaking and thrusts of, say, African dance. The pelvis, the seat of sexual desire and reproduction, is engaged only as support to the rest of the body, and contact with the floor is limited primarily to the feet. Such avoidances suggest a distaste for our animal nature and the earth with all its heathen associations and a predilection for a weightless and romanticized otherworldliness. An idealized and taut vertical order has replaced natural functions of the body. No surprise that when dancer and choreographer Vaslav Nijinsky strayed from classical vocabulary in *Le Sacre du printemps* in 1913, prolonging feral contact with the floor, his unorthodoxy contributed to an ensuing riot.

Folk dance, not designed for spectators but for participants, is geared toward the working class. These festive, social events provide a welcome break originally from work in the field and later the factory and the office. Folk dances come with explicit instructions — for instance, when to take hold of a partner's hand and when to spin. One need not undergo a rigorous training to carry out movements as is required by ballet, making folk dance accessible to a wide segment of the population. Folk dance intends as its prime goal neither to demonstrate the beauty of the form nor to entertain others. Rather, participants gather to engage in a socially approved activity, amicable meetings that promote fraternizing and, for some, the search for a potential romantic partner.

Although few would scorn or find any harm with social dances, there's a long history of dances arriving on the scene, only to be considered initially offensive or crass by the cultural elite. Though hard to believe today, a nineteenth century dance manual came with the warning that waltzing could lead to prostitution.[3] Tango, which originated in Argentine bordellos, would never be performed by any well-respecting citizen — that is, until the dance crossed the ocean to Europe where its bold sensuality was celebrated, absolving it of its former ignoble reputation. Hip-hop has undergone a similar transformation. Perceived initially as a threat, largely because the dance was developed by inner city black youth, a group susceptible to both racism and classism, the growing embrace by pop culture and dance companies such as Rennie Harris's PUREMOVEMENT has helped legitimize the form and shift focus away from its origins to the physical skills demanded by the dance.

Modern dance arose, in part, as a political statement against the classism of ballet. As an affront to its values, modernists did away with much that had been central to classical tradition. Off with shoes and corset (Isadora Duncan), off with music closely allied to set choreography (Merce Cunningham), and off with stylized form altogether (Yvonne Rainer). With the West increasingly industrialized and ripped apart by a series of wars during the twentieth century, modernism rooted itself in rebellion against an aesthetic norm, artists seeking expression closer to the changing values of working class people.

But much modern dance, too, practices its own form of elitism, preferring, similar to ballet, a fit and able body. When Ann Cooper Albright became wheelchair bound as a result of spinal degeneration, instead of saying goodbye to her choreography career, she brought her disfigured body onto the stage. "As a dancer, I am a body on display. As a body on display, I am expected to reside within a certain continuum of fitness and bodily control, not to mention sexuality and beauty. But as a woman in a wheelchair, I am neither expected to be a dancer nor to position myself in front of an audience's gaze. In doing this performance, I confronted a whole host of contradictions both within myself and within the audience."[4]

Maia Scott, who is blind, encountered similar prejudice in her pursuit of dance during grade and high school, her physical difference proving too great for many. "I've had ballet and dance all my life and feel both lucky and cursed with this truth. Lucky, I feel, because it has helped me spatially as a person who cannot see. On the other hand, I feel cursed because I let ballet and dance teach me to hate and despise and abuse my body."[5]

Although there has been a gradual shift in recent years, most professional dancers are expected to retire by around age forty, their bodies viewed as less beautiful and able than those a decade or two younger. Unlike forms such as the Japanese dance, butoh, which advocates small movements and an intense inward attention, much modern dance prefers a fast pace and large, Olympian gestures. Exceptions such as the Liz Lerman Dance Exchange exist. In defiance of ageism, Lerman's company, which she refers to as "cross-generational," recruits those who have retired from dance, including those in their sixties and seventies, some trying the discipline for the first time.

Equal Opportunity

CI radicalizes dance on numerous fronts. CI welcomes all, regardless of ability, race, age, class, or any other distinguishing quality. Be it a jam or a class, no one is discouraged from carrying their lethargic or sprightly body onto the floor. All that's needed is a willingness to take that initial step. When Scott discovered CI in college, she was "reduced to tears of bliss. I finally found a form of dance that innately took me for who I am, both blind and overweight."[6] The recognition that differently-abled individuals are as apt to engage in dance has spawned a wave of jams, classes, and performance companies featuring persons with mixed abilities. Wheelchair bound persons with paralysis, multiple sclerosis, or any other distinguishing physical challenge need not be excluded from entering the realm of dance and developing kinesthetic abilities.

Regardless of ability, and with CI not nearly as virtuosic as ballet, a Contacter need not train daily for years to perfect movements before engaging with a partner and reaping benefits. It's not uncommon for an experienced mover to partner with a beginner, CI welcoming refined skill alongside raw, unseasoned attempts. Though practiced by professional dancers, like folk dance, CI is also accessible to a broad segment of the population who may never attend a series of formal classes or step onto a stage, preferring instead to dance for socializing, developing physical skills, expanding awareness, or other reasons. This degree of accessibility is significant. Broadening the base for dance educates more people about the discipline, ensuring an appreciation and audience for the art. This is important because many art organizations have witnessed an alarming decline in attendance, due, in part, to younger generations' lack of education and exposure to the arts. The benefits that come from partaking in a physical art, developing one's body kinesthetically, proprioceptively, and expressively, learning the nuances of one's body and tapping into its wisdom, can be experienced by computer analysts, astrophysicists, housewives, carpenters, social workers, and so on, people whose dancing might otherwise be limited to events such as weddings and nightclubs, which rarely offer a safe, explorative

The dance floor as even playing field.

venue. Additionally, these people may choose to perform, allowing them to participate not only in a creative process, but also the steps involved in producing and staging a show.

AN EGALITARIAN SHUFFLE

CI reassembles the usual roles ascribed to individuals. Although a partnered dance, there is no leader and no follower. Instead, partners dance on equal footing and can break from usual societal expectations, dismantling prevalent hierarchical disparities based on gender, sexual preference, race, class, or ability. Not that such differences and their ramifications vanish miraculously once naked toes touch the floor. But as partners seek the common ground of the dance, within the press of flesh and play of motion, culturally reinforced habits, thoughts, and feelings can be jostled. In this new world of equality, partners can examine given roles and opt to abandon them for a revised relationship that no longer backs any one group into a ghetto. The dance acts as a pyre for burning unwelcome social debris and clearing space for a new social order based on mutual respect and equality. Such hierarchical reshuffling is not an abstract idea subject to debate and equivocation, but an experience rooted in felt sensation which can profoundly alter behaviors, perceptions, and community bonds.

This shift proves dramatic for men and women who may otherwise repeatedly find themselves in situations that reinforce traditional gender roles. In American society, men rarely experience physical contact and affection with other men, even between a father and son, in which handshakes and hugs are typically brief. Even contact sports like football and soccer, which emphasize physical touch, are limited to quick, aggressive pats, slaps, and shoves, nothing akin to the prolonged closeness of CI. Generally, men are applauded for actions that demonstrate their ability to take control of a situation and assert a grab for power. Relatively few activities promote close ties and supportive alliances. Gentleness and nurturing are not culturally reinforced, and those exhibiting such behavior may be pejoratively labeled feminine or another derogatory term.

Similarly, women generally receive kudos for showing deferential, docile natures and accentuating their visual beauty. Women are expected to maintain their appearance, their worth diminishing with wrinkles and graying hair. A prize on the arm of a man, a woman is applauded for not challenging the status quo and maintaining harmony, be it in the home or workplace. A woman who does otherwise, speaking out or asserting herself, is often suspect, denigrated as being manly or bitchy.

These portrayals demonstrate our society's gender stereotypes, defining masculine and feminine within a very narrow band. The advent of feminism has significantly impacted not only how men and women see themselves and each other, but also what behavior is publicly acceptable. CI further erases socially reinforced differences, with qualities such as gentleness, nurturing, daring, and strength becoming territory not exclusive to one gender but acceptable in whomever chooses to embrace it — no incrimination whatsoever. In a dance that

Who leads? Andy Wichorek and Kelley Lane.

stresses mutuality rather than dominance and encourages playing with a range of impromptu behaviors, neither sex has to justify actions or vie for the position of top dog. With the cultural dictates of gender rules relaxed, each person gets to range into unfamiliar or, depending upon one's conditioning, forbidden territory, ventures that allow the forging of new skills, poise, and insights. Rather than neutering differences and rendering dancers sexless, Contacters can embody a wider range of behavior. Men can unashamedly revel in their tender side and women can demonstrate strength without resorting to polite or politic excuses for their brashness. Says Contacter Ron Estes, "I can just get in there with a man with a lot of body contact where I'm not provided a context for doing that unless it's framed as competitive or blatantly sexual. I've got more room to be a person who's a man that's not so prescribed by the gender discourses I'm immersed in. I get to experience more of my humanity."[7]

The unrestricted range of gender behavior attracted CI teacher Kristin Horrigan to the dance. Her initial exposure to CI coincided with reflecting on the scripts handed her by her parents; the dance offered an option unavailable in her family. She reflects, "I discovered Contact when I was about twenty and was working at figuring out who I wanted to be as a woman as opposed to how I was raised. I was drawn to it because it was a place where I could be strong. I was raised to be emotionally strong, but not physically strong and hardy. It was a place where I could develop that and be supported."[8]

With any partnered combination possible, the usual status attributed to social groups loosens, shifting the balance of power. Each combination contains its own charge and trips off a series of thoughts and feelings that may threaten security and beliefs. What if my partner thinks I am pushy? What if he/she doesn't want to dance with me because of my age, ethnicity, class, religion, or physical ability? What if I am lesbian/gay? With equality among partners one of its features, CI may mark one of the few occasions where a traditionally low-status person engages on equal footing with a person of higher social ranking. With neither partner demoted, the experience ultimately proves useful as a stage for a new social order. This staging lets individuals try out new behaviors and perceptions that can be integrated into their lives both on and off the dance floor. Dancing without the reigns of society's biases invites one home into the natural liberty of the personal body, a restoration and affirmation of worth that is not dependent on social positioning or the chance circumstances of birth.

SEEKING CONNECTIONS

Another radical value is CI's promotion of cooperation. I regard this as radical because capitalist countries only partially understand what it means for separate parties to get along. Capitalism regards individuality and winning through competition as beacons of achievement. Collective entitlement, shared vision, and interdependency are secondary. Success is obtained by standing out and proving oneself superior to others, be it through possessions, knowledge, or skill, all of which provide access to power. Reward coincides with rising in rank, a hierarchical structure which means leaving others behind.

Much of our education concentrates on developing skills with an emphasis on competition, be it for sport, business, science, or the arts. Many buy into the belief that resources and rewards are limited, that it's better to vie for the goods and leave others in our wake, rather than find ways to thrive collectively amid mutual support. Interpersonal skills, when given attention, are directed towards civility, often manifesting superficially — a lowest common denominator, not genuine respect, mutuality, and deep accord. We are not taught how to reach towards another in bona fide appreciation nor shown how to create substantive reciprocal relationships. Nor are we taught to seek and value whatever unfamiliar qualities we believe dwell beyond our skin, yet in actuality may reside within ourselves as well, in dark corners or unmapped regions. Even when collaboration is essential, often the team's purpose is to surpass another team or single opponent. These relationships stress identifying each other's differences, classified as either strengths or weaknesses, and then jockeying for a position of advantage.

This competitive model, so prevalent in capitalism, conditions us to readily distrust others, to view them as nemeses. Acts of kindness, help, or support are rarely ends in themselves, but often suspect, viewed as strategy toward later gain. Even as it applies to romance, maintaining compatibility once the mad glow of attraction fades may leave many couples fumbling in the dark.

Forming solid alliances wherein the interests and particular qualities of all parties are supported, equitable, and welcome is a rarity. Yet this very correlative dynamic of mutual respect, a meeting ground, forms the foundation of CI. All partners provide pivotal contributions — in many ways fulfilling the feminist dream that values all and demeans none. Remarkably the dance not only uses, but builds upon, differences. Qualities which may have sprouted from congenital or cultural circumstances constitute the raw, neutral material for the dance. It's up to each partner to

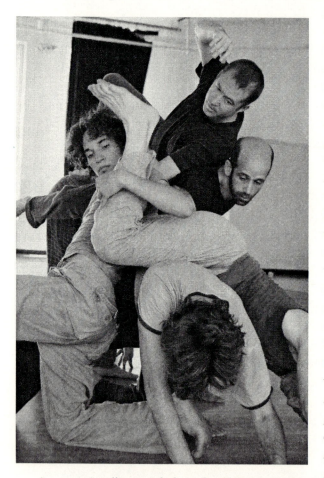

A cooperative alliance: (*clockwise from left*) Eric Ortega, Rob Smith, Ken Manheimer, Kelley Lane (*partly pictured*) and Robbie Kinter.

shuffle tempo, shift weight, yield to awkwardness, to do what is necessary in the moment to let go of expectations about the dance and honor a genuine communication. It's up to every dancer to initiate a dance, to introduce movement and encourage the same in a partner, and maintain a lively connection. If a dance is limited to the hands, can partners sustain the attention well enough to plumb the palm, the back of the hand, and each finger for nuances?

In being receptive and welcoming the diverse and changing dimensions of the dance, dancers do not perceive a quality as a strength or weakness, or good or bad. Every quality weaves its frayed or smooth thread into the composition of the dance, providing the timbre, the rhythm, the texture, the take and the give. Maybe the dance is riddled by bumps and grinds, maybe subtly shifting muscles. Maybe dancers sprint across the floor or perhaps they crawl shoulder to shoulder. Gestures and moods, intention and inattention rarely stay the same, but constantly mutate through sweat and stretch, breath and weight, as bodies flip upside down or lurch in a roll. What gets lugged or tossed into the dance effects the quality of the movements, manifesting as the dance itself. One dance may be The Dance of Unmaking History, another The Dance Where I Laugh at My Own Shortcomings, yet another A Dance of Tumbles or The Dance with My Rival.

The aim of CI is not to prove oneself better than others, be it your partner or fellow dancers. The dance provides a meeting where two or more bodies cough up differences and seek commonalities. The dance births a world wherein partners alternate roles, sovereign entity with commoner, an acclaimed dancer with a newcomer, a daredevil with the cautiously wary. Individuals may glide through a versatile resume that defies holding fast to any one position. Though some may initially fear such close collaboration and seeming loss of identity, only able to see the union as a dissolution of individuality, the dynamic encourages assertion, not passivity; evolution, not annihilation; diversity, not homogeneity. No one partner yields total power to the other. The partnership is not about compromising identity nor about submitting to a role, but about finding a balance — and if none exists at the start of a dance, dancers must establish it without sacrificing individual differences.

Creative collaboration and shared support: Nathan Long, Cheryl Pallant, and Robbie Kinter.

The dance holds center court, not particular dancers. Some may distinguish themselves stylistically from fellow practitioners, but if no relationship forms, the partners likely will loose interest and terminate the dance.

In many ways, CI epitomizes the ultimate win-win situation, no one partner losing self or dominion, or not for long. Each partner constantly plays with the ever-shifting balance, the center rolling across the floor, over a hip, or hoisted up onto a partner's shoulders. The dance is not only a distinctive me with a distinctive you, but a generative we, the dance a third entity swinging between letting go and holding on.

SYNERGY

The relationship between partners is one of interdependence, one person's moves immediately impacting the other. Here's where Paxton's ideas of mass, gravity, and momentum appear, and Newton's third law of motion, in which every action provokes an equal or opposite reaction, which I mentioned in Chapter 1. An individual movement, the kinetic force, prompts a parallel reaction. One dancer's balance leads to greater balance in the partnership. Or perhaps one's clumsiness leads to a thwarted or novel connection. I shift; you falter. I hold; you resist, or stay in place. You land on my back; my knees soften and spring with the impact.

It is this dynamic of interdependence that is so extraordinary. The close alliance between give and take without the presence of competition and struggle for dominance is a rare dynamic. CI omits antagonism and aggression — other than in play. One neither jockeys for dominance nor abides carte blanche to the dictates of an authority, be it to a group or an individual. The dance promotes, to use Buddhist monk Thich Nhat Hanh's term, a deep awareness of "interbeing,"[9] a recognition of our interdependency and interconnectedness, where seemingly individual energies emerge and merge to create a flow greater than any one person. Contacters open to the mystery of the unfolding moment, not doing, not action, not goal, not even the crafting of beauty. The dance focuses on the meeting of bodies, the creative and authentic negotiation of masses in shared space. Coexisting bodies establish their own rules, which may last a few minutes or the duration of the dance, rules not discussed beforehand (although some partners may do this), but accessed through the felt, living body. This dynamic may appear utterly lawless; on the other hand, it allows those rare occasions when the body asserts its own poetic dominion and inherent motion, astir with its own peculiar impulses and waves of energy.

It is noteworthy that this very freedom causes many of us, regardless of cultural origin, such difficulty in learning the dance, because we are so used to carrying out or struggling against the demands of others. This difficulty made an unwieldy appearance during a CI class in Hong Kong comprised largely of Chinese students. Contrary to my expectations, it wasn't touch with which they had difficulty, as is often the case with American students, but the invitation to improvise. Accustomed to the stringent rules of China which emphasizes the good of the collective, often at the expense of the individual, influencing

Interdependence: Cheryl Pallant and Robbie Kinter.

everything from housing to eating to creating art, they consistently stumbled with the direction to think on their own. They readily leaned into one another to establish a contact point, and as long as I narrated instructions for crossing their bodies' landscapes, they capably performed the dance. But once the instructions dropped off, so, too, did the dance, which within minutes slowed to a complete halt.

Similarly, when choreographer Vladimir Angelov initially came from Bulgaria to the United States with intensive ballet training, CI baffled him. "Never had I danced without shoes. For the first several weeks of CI, I was deeply confused. What's the point of this dance, I kept asking."[10] Used to interpreting choreography, carrying out the wishes of another, he struggled with the instruction to feel in the moment, to map out terrain for himself, and to connect with another body.

These dancers illustrate what somaticist Don Hanlon Johnson explains as the way ideas impose themselves upon us, frequently outside

Continuously reshaping: Isabel Halley, Corinne Mickler, Sarah LaBanna Fraser, and Azalia Smith.

the conscious mind. "We are gripped by ideologies. The dominant values of our culture insinuate themselves into our neuromuscular responses, shaping our perception of the world. Altering the morbid dynamics of our culture requires us to loosen their hold upon our flesh."[11] Every experience imprints itself upon our cells, influencing our thought and actions, the more dramatic and repetitive ones literally shaping our flesh, appearing through posture, movement, and responsiveness.

A PERSONAL STUDY

Some of us may have few outlets other than CI for creative, kinesthetic expression — no place for a body to call its own, no place where an investigative body can sort through influences, choosing to keep or modify some and discard others. It's no wonder so many Contacters commit heartily to the form; it may be their only vehicle for connecting deeply with their bodies, locating the social knots and chains, unfettering themselves from expectations of family, work, and society, and developing creativity. By bringing into awareness which habits and patterns rule them, CI can loosen their grip and point out options.

German Contacter Andrew Wass reflects his CI experience in the way he walks unafraid with newly found confidence among pedestrians. "Before in crowds, I would always give others more space, negotiating them more slowly, often doing so with fear. You know those times when you almost bump into someone and that little shuffle dance happens, both go left then right, then left again? Embarrassed smiles on both sides. Now I am more likely just to pick a direction and trust the other person to take care of themselves."[12] His more confident attitude while walking demonstrates his right to claim space, a right many may give up habitually as a result of low status, fear, or some other form of self-denigration.

The personal body is the very site where politics manifest and, therefore, the site where change is possible. To further quote Johnson:

Those who have best understood how to control human communities — charismatic religious and political leaders, advertising consultants, thought-control scientists — know that the body is not inevitable, a given. Its tastes can be dulled, its ocular range narrowed, its emotional reactions channeled in one direction rather than another. The supple newborn can be trained in mechanical behavior so that once grown up it will react to its world predictably and passively buying the right products and voting for the right candidates. Shaping the flesh becomes crucially important in the organization and maintenance of power.[13]

By tuning in to beliefs while noting bodily responsiveness, we see how cultural ideals live in our body, some supporting our actions and others inhibiting, even strangling, our best intentions to connect with our self and another. Once acknowledged, we can then ask what it means to reciprocate respect, not an imperious, empty decree aimed at face-saving, but a genuine honoring. In the shared space of bodies crossing boundaries into another's jurisdiction, what holds us back from heartfelt diplomacy and participation in a dance of mutual creativity? Which movements, sensations, and awarenesses do we ostracize and which receive invitations to the dance? Every movement offers an opportunity for renewal, expression, validation, digression, and egression — possibilities beyond the scope of anyone's imagining, beyond sexism, racism, ageism, classism, any-ism that denigrates rather than praises, that puts down rather than uplifts, that chips away rather than celebrates individual differences and liberties.

To come home to the body and live neither in the margins nor in exile is a profound political statement of one's rights. CI contributes to a settled entitlement that tends toward greater generosity and less susceptibility to the manipulations of others. By providing routes to carry out wishes, CI reinforces empowerment, raising levels of respect, discernment, and trust for all. In the often twisting path that leads back home, full of frailties and obstacles, the dance reinforces compassion by revealing how every action carries repercussions, repercussions that are conjoined. It lets one look in the mirror and see not only a distinctive face, but also the traits we share in common.

QUESTIONS

- Who are the dancers you typically dance with? How are they like you? Who are the dancers you typically avoid? How are they different from you? What skills could you develop to bridge the differences?

- When do you stop listening to yourself and listen more to your partner to the point of imbalance? Who are the dancers you do this with? What do they have that you don't? What is an appropriate balance?

- Think about your early dance classes. Did they reflect diversity or were they homogenous?

- Are there certain partners with whom you dance more generously with than others? With whom do you make concessions, and who challenges your patience? What are the qualities of each type of dancer? In what small or large ways do you manifest those same qualities?

EXERCISES

Teachers and Learners

Dance with persons you perceive as less experienced than you. However, don't approach the dance as lacking. Instead, consider these partners your teachers, with valuable experience and insight into the dance. Their approach to the dance differs from yours. Learn from them. Note how their bodies convey specialized kinesthetic knowledge, how they work with balance, shifts in weight, and control. Learn their particular ways of moving. Follow their leads and prompts closely. Note your responses, be it impatience, resistance, fatigue, judgments. Which responses of yours interfere with having a shared, connected dance with an awareness of the richness of the present moment? How are the qualities your teachers manifest latent in you?

If you are the less experienced one, be aware that your partner is looking for your special knowledge and is listening to your body attentively.

Welcome grace and awkwardness. Note how your partner's responsiveness influences your movements and the dance.

Variations: Go from dancer to dancer, hunting for a lesson, a particular quality in the dance, a specific movement. Turn the hunt into a journey.

Selection by Quota

Divide dancers into two groups by clothing, for instance patterned tops and unpatterned tops or sleeved and sleeveless shirts. Decide on a length of time, about an hour, for this exercise. Designate one group the Majority, the other the Minority, and one person the Watcher. The Majority selects a secret gesture, such as backward roll or raised right arm, and shares this information with the Watcher.

Both groups go to separate areas on the floor to dance. Each group should have enough time to let their movements evolve into a group synergy. Groups may divide into duets, trios, and so forth. Alternate partners frequently. The Watcher observes the Minority group. The aim is to get participants to cross an invisible boundary and dance together. Those in the Minority must be invited to dance with the Majority. This takes place only when a Minority dancer executes the secret gesture by accident, observation, or another method. Once the gesture is manifested, the Watcher calls out that person's name who is then welcome to dance with the Majority. Those in the Minority can try to dance with those in Majority, without the call of their names, but Majority members must refuse partnering with them. Time will likely run out before the two groups blend completely. The Watcher announces the end. All come together to reflect on what transpired.

Dancing as the Other

Define some characteristics of a dancer whose style of dancing is unlike yours. Discuss those qualities with a partner. Listen, in particular, for admiration, envy, and judgmental remarks. Notice how you phrase your comments or what you withhold. Walk around the dance floor and begin to embody the qualities in this other dancer. Manifest them in your pace, your carriage, your facial expression, your interaction with the space. Meet up with your partner and engage in a dance while maintaining those qualities. What new movements emerge?

Taking Sides

Either with one other person or a group, discuss qualities that make a successful CI dance. Think of specific dancers and identify the qualities that arise from dance skill and those rooted in personality. Discuss how these qualities get celebrated in society. Now identify qualities that are considered unsuccessful in the dance. Generate a dance in which you manifest the qualities that are not celebrated.

5

The Relating Body:
Alienation and Orientation

*We cannot bear connection. This is our malady. We must
break away, and be isolate. We call that being freed, being
individual. Beyond a certain point, which we have reached,
it is suicide.*
— D.H. Lawrence

*The illusion that we are separate from one another is an
optical delusion of our consciousness.*
— *Albert Einstein*

With cell phones, email, faxes, and the like, now more so than
ever, we have a host of readily available technology to ensure easy access
to friends, family, and colleagues who may live as close as a few miles
or as far away as a continent. Despite such easy access to communication, a nagging feeling of isolation, a disconnect from our surroundings, and an emptiness bordering on alienation persist for many of us.
We manage the technology well enough and know which buttons to
press in what order, but when it comes to extending ourselves genuinely
to another, feeling inclusive, in kinship with fellow beings, and finding
a hospitable place on earth, the gadgetry proves ineffectual. We fumble for the right words or don't even try. We offer a hand and then
retract it with a cursory reason. Perhaps out of fear or defensiveness,
we avoid any sign of so-called touchy-feelyness, disparaged as evidence
of weakness. Instead we resort to safe, common topics or simple acts
that forge easy, superficial ties, attending a movie together or discussing
the arrival of the latest coffee shop. There is great value in such ties,

95

but when they constitute the majority of our exchanges to the neglect of substantive and heartfelt ones, much of who we are gets ignored and compromised.

When Contacters come together, they thrive on ample opportunities for connection, welcoming with little hesitation the chance to be in touch literally with fellow dancers. Ready to yield and give weight, they enter the flock of moving bodies on the dance floor, rolling, shuffling, or leaping onto the back of a ready or unsuspecting partner. Duets, trios, quartets, and larger groups continually form, dissolve, and reassemble into new arrangements as separate bodies explore their fit into a moving puzzle. A soft, sensual floor-bound dance may erupt into a flurry of interlocking slippery limbs or a prance across the space. A comedic knock on the head may interrupt a sweaty exertion. A shin meets an elbow. An armpit encounters a thigh. A body stumbles into and lands or strides up to another body. There is no doubt here that bodies are connecting.

RESTORATIVE TOUCH

With a vigor frequently reserved for sport, Contacters immerse themselves in animated exchanges, traveling from one dance to the next, sometimes stopping only upon exhaustion. As if opportunities for contact during the dance aren't enough, when dancers finally take a break, they may lay their weary bodies down not in separate chairs, not even in separate quadrants of the floor, but sometimes draped across each other in a tangle of limbs.

This willing embrace of touch comes as no surprise to bodyworker Deane Juhan who sees our society as touch deprived and touch phobic, despite innumerable physical and psychological benefits derived from touch. Common knowledge to bodyworkers, whether they practice Myofascia Release Work, Body-Mind Centering, Alexander Technique, or Rolfing, is that touch, the rich sensory event of flesh meeting the presence of another, is one of the most effective ways to generate ease, reinforce natural immunities, increase self-awareness, establish synaptic links, and shift energy — essentially to awaken the body's potential on multiple levels. Much of this information gets lost on a society that cannot separate touch from sex and romance. Those with this narrow understanding of touch have difficulty recognizing nonsexual touch and see touch outside of romance as transgressive. Safeguards are essential to keep bona fide abusers at a distant, yet the worthy effort to keep touch safe prevents many of us from learning to distinguish and benefiting from wholesome types of touch. Those not in a romantic relationship may go without physical contact altogether. Its absence may leave even the healthiest among us to flail in an ocean of activity without a life vest, out of reach with what is helpful, nurturing, and life-giving.

Numerous studies over the past several decades show to what degree touch is crucial to survival. Although they may otherwise receive adequate health care, orphaned infants in intensive care units who do not get cuddled or stroked on a daily basis waste away, unable ever to put on necessary weight during a period in their maturation when weight gain is crucial. Many of these infants as well as older children similarly deprived develop life threatening diseases, mental retardation or stunted growth, some succumbing to death.[1]

Receiving proper care during early life is critical for the growing child, but it is similarly indispensable for adults. Says Juhan, "Touch is one of the principal elements necessary for the successful development and functional organization of the central nervous system, and is as vital to our existence as food, water, and breath."[2] Quite literally, touch keeps us in touch, allowing us to forge necessary connections between ourselves and other, refining perceptions, providing valuable insight and ease with our place in the world. It lays a bridge between where we end and another begins. Yet many adults live alone or, if living with families, limit contact to an occasional hug. Contacter and Alexander Technique teacher Jennifer Stanger notes, "We touch primarily during transitions, when we greet people and when we say goodbye. When you start to dance and touch, then you get to know that person. That's the real them.... The rest of society has it backward and Contact corrects it to a better or more authentic way."[3]

When we touch, we are utilizing one of the largest organs of the body, the skin. Housing millions of nerve endings, skin is the largest, most varied, and most constantly active source of sensations in the body.[4] Covering the entire surface of the body, this adaptable outer layer provides us with a distinct shape, at the same time separating us from the rest of the world. Skin lets us know when we've bumped up against the world with its myriad scents, textures, and shapes, helping us define those encounters. Paradoxically, as much as skin distinguishes us from everything else, it simultaneously ushers the world in, blurring the very boundaries it maintains. Whatever is outside — sunlight, car horns, rain, heat, another body — alights upon and passes through the filter of our skin and nerves. Such events not only inform us about the world, but our reactions to them simultaneously inform us about who we are. The sensory reach of our skin connects us to our surroundings.

The touch applied in massage and other forms of bodywork aim toward healing, restoring a lapse in balance and wholeness, the body acting in concert with itself. Deft hands work towards releasing tensions, generating heat, restoring the pliancy of traumatized connective tissue, redirecting energy, and encouraging flow blocked by a buildup of stressors. Touch provokes an event of perception, bringing attention to an area which may be neglected or overused. The contact awakens the body to itself, pointing out habitual patterns embedded in the connective tissue resistant to change, slow to respond, or eager for relief from overuse. Rooted in the present, touch points toward the possibility of new ways of feeling, thinking, responding, and moving through the day.

Moving Energy

Touch helps generate new synaptic links and relieve worn ones, simultaneously supporting change on energetic levels. These energetic levels, referred to as *prana* in Sanskrit, *ki* in Japanese, *chi* in Chinese, are a system of subtle energies that course throughout the body and the universe. Westerners typically accept Newton's mechanistic, matter-based model of the body, a series of interlocking parts that function (or falter) and can be replaced. However, more and more health-care professionals embrace Einstein's understanding of all matter as energy. Dr. Richard Gerber refers to the molecular arrangement of the physical body as a complex network of interwoven energy fields. He explains, "The energetic network, which represent the physical/cellular framework, is organized and nourished by 'subtle' energetic systems which coordinate the life-force with the body."[5] One way to impact the life-force is through touch. Touch is a direct conduit to energy, and how we move it determines how it moves us.

When connective tissue, the collagen fabric extending throughout our body, gets manipulated, it stimulates a shift in the body's invisible energetic fields. Science researcher Robert Ochsman refers to connective tissue as piezoelectric, meaning that it generates electric fields when compressed or stretched. Movement of any part of the body — muscle, bone, skin, blood vessel, and so forth — generates dynamic electrical fields that spread through the surrounding tissues. Habituated movements stiffen and dry out the gel-like substance of connective tissue which thrives on a continuous flow of information to keep it active and vital. When this flow is reduced as a result of a change in the daily routine or from physical or emotion injury, Ochsman states, "the mechanical properties of the tissue are affected, awareness may decrease, and pain may arise. Repeated use of the same muscles and nerves dries and stiffens the body, making receptivity and responsiveness increasingly difficult."[6] Such stiffness is common among the elderly, many of whom accept inflexibility as an inevitable consequence of aging. It is also apparent in younger people who rarely exercise and maintain a sedentary lifestyle. Recognizing the mind-body connection, psychologist Ashley Montagu sees a direct link between an active lifestyle and a flexible mind. He refers to inflexible attitudes, which are not age-dependant, as "psychosclerosis," basically "the hardening of the mind" or the inability to learn anything new.[7]

One way the body enlivens and renews itself is through touching, applying pressure, and moving — the very actions that take place during CI. The direct somatic interaction reminds the body of itself and its myriad abilities, the stimulation also moistening and revitalizing the connective tissue. Introducing a range of movement not only hydrates tissue, it also helps release trapped toxins and metabolites. With the physical release comes an energized calm which yields increased awareness and access to a greater range of behavior and motion. Significantly, where the body goes, so too goes the mind. Increasingly, scientists and health-care professionals find this connection hard to ignore.[8]

Consequently, moving the body moves the mind and vice versa. Stepping outside usual habits and bounds to connect with the physical and primordial self, the body revitalizes through varying movement, whether prompted by a health-care practitioner, dance partner, or oneself. As we dance, movement is uncovered, cajoled, permitted, and released, not constrained or manipulated. Partners can run wild like children racing across an open field, dropping to the ground in gleeful exhaustion or stopping to gather a pocketful of stones, their smooth or rough, uneven surfaces turned over again and again with their fingers. The dance is a play with touch, motion, rhythm, timbre, and texture, movement arising like any other natural bodily function which is not manufactured or restrained to fit a preconception. We may sprint across the floor in wonderment, slowing when a shoulder presses into our ribs, the contact eliciting heat, a turn towards our partner, or a spiraling away. The movement may be spacious or subtle, fluid or dissonant, isolating or relational. We may imitate the walk of a chicken, luxuriantly recline across our partner, or grab hold of a hip for steadiness as we slide to the floor. Deviating from our usual tendency to inhibit motion to fit some standard, be it etiquette or aesthetics, CI urges us to take part in a dance of our entire being, no limb, organ, or function of the body set apart and denied its share of breath. Not only do we carry out familiar movements, but we are encouraged to try something new, be it our neck jutting forward and backward or climbing atop a partner's outstretched thigh.

CI's focus on touch and an expansive range of movement stimulates nerve pathways and generates new connections. The body awakens not only to itself, but also to the environment of which it is part. It is hard to ignore a partner brushing against us, stretching our skin or pressing into the density of our muscle and bone. It is hard to ignore the heat of another body mixing with the heat of our own. Whether the movements are large and athletic or as simple as a the back of a hand grazing a forearm, the touch and motion encourages us to inhabit ourselves more fully, to reside in the present moment, to sense and feel. We are forced to establish a relationship with current circumstances, not a fabricated notion that can create distance and unsettling divisions. There is little room for reflection when a 150-pound body flings itself at us or encircles us like a ribbon tightening into a bow. Each response to the presence of another moving body connects us to the terra firma of bodies. In the process, alienating distances abbreviate or disappear altogether.

CI requires that dancers constantly change movements and shift

A puzzling fit: Page Ghaphery, Brad Stoller, and Jennifer Stanger.

their weight and balance with partners. We step back to form an arch when a partner presses into our chest. We fold down as his weight collapses upon us. If we slip off our partners, we extend our limbs against the floor to soften the blow of the impact. This practice of constant sensing and adapting to touch reinforces the ease with which we meet our partners, but also influences how we encounter many circumstances which, on first glance, seem unrelated to dance. Dancing not only sensitizes me to my partner, but after dancing, too, I walk with a lighter and more fluid step. If I stumble over a vine, my body does not tense; I recover my balance quickly. If I receive distressing news, I feel the pierce of sadness or thud of disappointment and then move on as best I can. On the dance floor and off, I feel mutable in body and attitude which allows me to glide with events, to adapt to circumstances, not resist them. Energy and motion are continuous, not a logjam with possible negative repercussions.

Fluid Connection

Although there are some who embrace CI for its therapeutic value, restoring health is not its aim. The dance is more open-ended, neither partner assigned the role of healer or client. Certainly, the roving touch of CI can unblock energy stoppages and encourage flow, which lends itself to feeling whole, but the focus of the dance is on the physical and creative dialogue between dancers. Partners focus on the play of their relationship, riding the waves of sensation and momentum to uncover the possibilities of a moving, improvising body encountering another body in motion.

Touch, the ever-moving contact point, is core to CI, the seed from which the dance sprouts. A nonverbal signal, an event that is both solitary and shared, touch directs attention. The contact points provide the stable yet mobile foundation upon which the dance is based. Dancers communicate through this elemental tie, a sensate act dependant on the tangible presence of another. Relationship is key. Does a partner thrust his entire weight upon you or only a leg? Does he

Ease in stillness: Susan Singer and Keith Winston.

balance from your pelvis, pivoting from side to side like a door hinge, one careless move instigating a topple to the floor? If the dance takes your partner to the floor, do you provide an arm's leveraging to keep yourself up or do you go to the floor, too? The bond of touch and coexistence of bodies, along with the information and energy exchanged in motion, builds an alliance that surpasses ordinary interactions. Partners do not discuss the weather nor eye each other with suspicion. Rather, bodies orbit side by side on the dance floor, following parallel and intersecting trajectories that spontaneously and mysteriously appear. Kinetic bodies engage with one another, skin pressed against skin, weave against seam, force confronting force, a conspicuous connection that highlights surfaces and hints toward depth and hidden complexities. Such a relationship cannot be taken lightly. The compression of weight accentuates the entirety of the body, tissue and bone, breath and cells, thought and motion, subtle energy and matter. Even a skim of the surface stirs the waters and silt below. When a hip bone presses into our flesh or hair flies in our faces, the stimuli compels acknowledgment and response.

Using physical contact rather than words, partners uncover pathways of flesh in endless combinations, across the shoulders and pressing into the collar bone, between the legs and pivoting off the tailbone, passages ornamented by cotton, nylon, spandex, hair, sweat, muscle, angles, contours, soft fleshy spots, and hard bony ridges. The less tangible details of emotion and thought texture the connection further. Sensation brings a dancer back again and again to the turmoil and flow of the dance, partners diving into the stream of Being, our organismic nature, histories pressed into flesh, the potential of each moment unwinding and revealing bodies as a mix of energy and matter, form continually reforming. Moving bodies planted in space together — feet, hands, or forearms sometimes vying for the same few inches — make it impossible to ignore the influence of another body, make isolation and alienation a remote reality.

Touch is anything but a casual occurrence. With touch core to the dance, the quality of the connection is pivotal. The dancer must determine instantly whether the stimulus of the touch and its momentum is harmful, helpful, or neutral. How to respond? Redirect or encourage it? Lean in or pull away? Maintain your center of gravity or veer toward its perimeter? Widen your stance or stand on one leg? Most dancers lean towards touch that is supportive, trusting, and responsive, demonstrating a high degree of alertness and listening. Hardened bodies, resistant flesh that demonstrates little elasticity and receptivity, armored by the tribulations of living, tend to exhibit a limited range of listening and motion, but instead are preoccupied by internalized dramas that play repeatedly with little regard for the stream of new information offered in the present moment. Such dancers may knock into partners, the contact points banging and bouncing along like rocks loosened from a cliff in rapid descent toward the valley. Conversely, dancers devoted to attending their own kinesthetic journeys, openly investigating their somatic history and its interface with others, learn how, for instance, to deepen a stretch or lengthen a muscle without strain. Such dancers find ways to remove defensive layers, results being greater pliancy, receptivity, and animation. Such dancers find ripples of muscles and less visible actions, a life-force undulating with movement possibilities. The dance may speed up or slow down, the space and time of motion elastic and intricate. Something as seemingly insignificant as a finger extending above the rest of the hand may assume dramatic stature. The dance is at its finest when partners actively listen to both the bold movements and the subtleties of tissue; the dance drags along when it returns again and again to a known, worn groove.

SUPPORT AND TRUST

When Contacters engage in the dance, support and trust work hand in hand. Whereas in many encounters, we reserve trust until provided evidence otherwise, CI partners by definition readily extend trust first, building a foundation that simultaneously generates support. Contacters look to meet the movements of each other, finding ways their bodies fit together, seeking a genuine dance that acknowledges the particulars of the moment. That partners encounter each other without goal or preconception allows the dance to rise to its potential. We offer our weight to partners or receive theirs. We find surfaces like a thigh or a pelvis or a shoulder from which to pivot, sharing motion and balance. And we do so without knowing what movement will follow, led only by the shared contact point and mutual trust.

Rare that we join together in naked, uncritical attention, exposing ourselves in the moment of Becoming. Rare that we grant space to ourselves and another to simply Be. Maybe a dance diva or an oversized fumbling toddler emerges on the dance floor. What matters is that the dance provides room enough for a full range of movements to emerge. Deep listening to the twitches and sighs, the lifts and pulls, the frenetic speed and the torpid stretches champions a more complete expression of life. In dancing at this depth of attention, where sensual being takes precedence, the fleeting stirrings of each person is welcomed and honored, no part alienated or sent into exile. Judging, inhibiting and holding, which reinforces division, is suspended; letting go and acknowledging promotes increased consciousness and rides along the waves of Being, the very material that is the foundation of CI.

Contacters are well aware of the responsibility that accompanies letting down our guard to open to the impromptu motion of the moment. For some, the exposure leaves them uncomfortably vulnerable; others value that same vulnerability. Remember that in many instances, Contacters may be meeting their partner for the first time on the dance floor. Acknowledging the lack of guile customary between partners, Contacter Richard Aviles explains, "Contact demands that if you're going to be that intimate with someone who you don't know, you give them the highest degree of respect, so it has that element of sacredness. I'm going to honor you as much as possible and not violate that trust that you're providing me to make yourself vulnerable to this movement."[9]

The dance imparts equal billing to parts we typically present to the world as well as the parts we may abandon or hide — or may not even know exist. For example, many of us left crawling behind in childhood, yet Contacters may find themselves on hands and knees alongside or

A wordless meeting: Corinne Mickler and Niall Jones.

beneath their partner. An embarrassed dancer might quickly return to her feet or she may recognize her mobility without judgment. Without judgment, not only do the walls within oneself break apart, but the barriers separating partners do, too. We are neither trembling timorously at the threshold of life nor collecting excuses as to why we cannot accept its invitation. Embracing the potential of the moment, we are instead like Goethe's Faust, who seeks a glimpse of his soul and says, "Now let me dare to open wide the gate/Past which men's steps have ever flinching trod."[10] We may crawl side by side, shoulder to shoulder, discover the solidity of the position, and then use it to propel ourselves over our partner's back. The crawl is not divorced from the rudimentary travail of childhood but provides a foundation from which to build movement. A dancer could shy away from the movement, shackled by its association, or use it to link to new experience. If the latter, dancers receive the gift of embodiment, increased energy, and spontaneity, life simmering as a multicourse meal, not a few stale crumbs. Dancers discover the value of being a body in motion with no plan other than to acknowledge and yield to itself and interact similarly

Fully relaxed and open to the world: Page Ghaphery and Jennifer Stanger.

with another, to note what appears as sound, image, thought, touch, or scent, to unearth the body of existence and reveal its molten magnificence.

The dance may alert us to a memory knocking at the door of awareness or provoke a slow promenade across the floor. The dance can strip away artifice to reveal a more raw, vulnerable side, Being in the moment of becoming, replete with all its contradictions and perplexities. The body is given permission to step outside usual conventions and invited to return to its nascent origins, its instinctive intelligence, cells dividing, breath inspiring, blood coursing, energy bursting or wafting into form and motion.

PURPOSEFUL PLAY

Add play to this already potent mix, the attitude often embraced and encouraged in this improvisational dance and the energy charges even further. Playing within CI widens the range of opportunities to connect with a partner. Play assumes innocence, supports investigative behavior, reserves judgment, sets aside differences such as race, sex, or class. Play contains levity, not estrangement. Play bends rules and reveals them as mutable, none sacrosanct. The crawl mentioned previously may instigate further childlike movements like clenched hands, a carefree lunge, a loss of balance. What matters in play is a willingness to try something new, to toss aside inhibitions, to suspend usual conclusions, to plunge into the unknown, to turn the familiar upside down. Play reserves judgment, tests limits and boundaries, and provides immediate feedback.

Play within CI helps dancers fix awareness on the present. Gesture, behavior, order, emotion, and thought can mingle, transmute, reorganize, and settle into a more fluid awareness. In the process, the ordinary mixes with the extraordinary, the common with the unusual — even a motion as basic as an arm extending toward the ceiling may contain these qualities. What had been locked in the past or sealed in an imagined future weaves itself into the texture of the dance. Unfortunately, play receives a bad rap in this country, considered folly and a sign of immaturity, whereas in countries like India, play receives high regard, exemplifying spirit and art. The ability to play (referred to as *lila* in Sanskrit) means one is participating in the cosmic dance of the universe, and those who play are readily tapping into its gifts. Play is not denigrated as immature behavior or the domain of children but appreciated as fruit of the gods.

Elbowing our habits and encouraging a roll, wriggle, and slide, CI positions us closer to the truths of our bodies. Play associated with CI moves us out from our isolation and preconceptions into a realm that is more panoptic. Mythologist Joseph Campbell says exhilaration often results from a playful embrace of what stands before us. "The play state and the rapturous seizures sometimes deriving from it, represent, therefore, a step toward than away from the ineluctable truth.... The world of play opens up possibilities that are inconceivable in the ordinary world."[11] Researchers a conclude that play is not childish but profoundly affect those who embrace it — which may explain why so

Mutual exploration of space: Robbie Kinter (*top*) and Dennis Chambers.

many Contacters are drawn to the form, regularly attending jams in their own town and traveling great distances to meet dancers from far away. The dance assumes transcendent stature, an isolated self communing with a more immense self. For anthropologist and psychologist Jean Houston, a colossal power generates from dancing, which connects to a universal participation. She explains, "In Africa gods are thought to be themselves dancers, frequency waves and rhythms that are closer to the great rhythms and patterns than our local selves. To dance, then, is to pray, to meditate, to enter in communion with the larger dance, which is the universe. And because the universe dances, as the Ghanian Yoruba priest explains, 'he who does not dance does not know.'"[12]

Exhilaration is one side effect of play, doors opening to new motion and expression, and, in turn, energy previously unavailable or unwelcome. Partners also discover that the playfulness of CI leads to relating, influence, convergence, empowerment, transcendence, wave upon a shore, wind upon a branch, flame against flicker, breath uncovering breadth. With awareness immersed in the moment, partners not limited by role or time or expectation step across thresholds of isolation and detachment, bonding in ways that frequently take them by surprise. CI teacher Alicia Grayson describes her awe with the dance as "an energy, a spirit that's moving through my partner and I. It's the mystery and magic and surprise, the not knowing, opening to something larger than what I think is going to happen in any moment."[13] Such inspiration fuels many a Contacter to leap, lift, carry out an unexpected series of movements, or settle into a deep stillness. I've witnessed Grayson in duets that seem destined for injury, one partner riding the other like a roller coaster with continuous twists and turns, rises and falls, yet her level of attentiveness and counterweight always keep them squarely on the side of safety.

Contacters find a balance between effort and effortlessness, giving but also taking, guiding and letting go. The composite of who we are, the past staring headlong at the present, selves swapping places, all stir into motion in a mutually supported and trusting relationship. CI teacher Shakti Andrea Smith finds sanctuary in dances where she "can

Glimpsing exhilaration: Veronica Ramon.

let go and find permission to be. There's something about that which brings out innocence and childlikeness. I see it in myself and others around me — a spiritual quality. I relate it to different meditation practices and to Buddhism where you're focusing in, and in that focusing, the mind quiets and, at the same time, opens up and widens. A greater awareness comes from that focus."[14] Such focus is not necessarily extraordinary in itself. But because we spend a majority of time disembodied, preoccupied with concerns taking us away from sensing and dwelling more fully in the emerging moment, the shift in attention feels profound. When we focus on the forthcoming moment, we are inviting our energies home, not sending them away in pursuit of some ideal. Yet many of us go neglectfully through the day distracted by fantasies about the future or nostalgia about the past. Perhaps we're imagining who we may meet at an upcoming conference or recalling a dinner that burned, both complicated further by judgments about them. Or while dancing, we're trying to predict the next moves or determine where in the studio we may end up. In essence, we're trying to manipulate circumstances to fit our preconceptions and desires, or vice versa, rather than opening our senses and accepting the moment as it is, inhabiting our body with all its strains and ease. Ignoring what hovers, perches, or sings in close vicinity can disrupt the balance that comes with attention anchored in the present moment. Ignoring what's close at hand infringes upon the conduits to available energy, perhaps closing the access entirely. Skillful attention and experience shows us how to establish equilibrium.

In attending to the moment without imposing an agenda upon it, we relate in new ways to ourselves and our partner. Things residing outside our usual perception range, the treasures buried in the unconscious and events transpiring at a nearby yet neglected distance, have an opportunity to step forth and catch our attention. The shift may yield an altered state, a result which psychologist Arnold Mindell attributes to a turning away from habitual attention toward the sensory perceptions we normally do not use. Referring to our senses and modes of consciousness as "channels," he explains how focusing on an unoccupied channel such as proprioception can create an altered state. Shifting how we focus our attention "stops the world, for intentionally feeling the world is more foreign to us than seeing."[15] With Contacters tuning in so keenly to touch, a sense typically receiving little daily attention and slighted in favor of sight, the switch in consciousness feels nothing short of dramatic.

Power lies in recognizing and residing in the here and now, allowing the body its due, accepting it and its environs as is. Mind does not attempt to exert control solely, but honors the many interdependent processes of the body. We step into ourselves and celebrate our organismic process, breath by breath, one drop of sweat after another. Referring to the innate wisdom of the body, choreographer Deborah Hay says about this type of attention, "Where I am is what I need cellularly."[16] An awareness riveted to the present, where we align with and participate in our surroundings, roots us to the richness of ourselves, the earth, and other, a type of attention that is profoundly simple, yet often fraught with numerous obstacles. Less egocentric and more expansive, such awareness alters consciousness — no small matter — affirming who we are in the ongoing process of becoming. This is not to say Contacters yield their will entirely to the dance. Effort, intention, and desire do not get poured down the nearest drainpipe without regard for outcome, with no one claiming responsibility for the direction of the dance. Rather, the dancer returns regularly to centeredness and grounding. The spine's axis, relaxed yet ready muscles, regular deep breaths, and attention focused but not fixated on the contact point provide a necessary steadiness in a situation whose rapid or faltering flux may land a dancer on her head. Centeredness, with an emphasis on elasticity, not rigidity, points out the routes between overly stressful exertions and more easily supportable actions.

A SELF AMONG SELVES

The self emerges as much more than a discrete, fixed entity bound by flesh and the many thoughts and feelings that dwell within conceptual walls. Though we call ourselves a given name which contributes to the illusion of a separate and static self, our bodies continually oxygenate, secrete, contract, reproduce, shed, and expand, performing a versatile range of complex processes, many undetectable to the eye. We may be the sole occupant of our car, but once we look beyond the plastic of the dashboard and the glass of the windshield, the road reveals a web of pavement with countless other vehicles racing or chugging alongside us. Be it tar or connective tissue, our matter dances ceaselessly with the matter of our partner and the environment of which we are part. In the course of the dance, self is revealed as a process both influencing and influenced by circumstances in a mutually responsive relationship to the world. Where then do we place the dividing line? The grassy median strip or the windshield? The loose threads of the cotton T-shirt or the end of the toenail? The dance provides a concretely irrefutable experience of a connection to something beyond our singularity.

When I find myself upside down on my partner, my hair and the rest of me slipping toward the floor, every nerve and fiber in my body is alerted to ensuring a solution that leads not to a concussion but to a soft landing. In those critical moments, I extend myself to my partner and the floor, synergy and cooperation between flesh and floor my greatest allies. Perceptual awareness widens and distances shrink as I extend my usual boundaries, the range of my senses expanding beyond my skin into another, a grounding not limited to my physical body. Even a gentle, less threatening situation awakens my reflexes. Whether I lift my gaze to meet my partner's or feel her weight press against my ribs, every movement, so close to skin and breath, is deeply personal, sharing clues about each other. Be it sweat or clenched muscles, feedback is immediate. Within seconds, my body reads hers and uncovers movement options. Maybe I follow a momentum already begun, or perhaps I introduce a new gesture or movement quality. Whichever of the many paths our sensitized bodies pursue, I get to articulate a wordless conversation that probes and participates in a world that includes me as an integral player.

With connections generating between self and environment, an entire host of lost and rudimentary behaviors, movements, emotions come to life. Physical systems blink in revival, rigidity melts into pliancy, breath deepens, and eyes glisten, not glaze over. We can greet fellow dancers with openness and enthusiasm, no longer braced defensively, cowering in neglect, or walking past indifferently; in turn, the world appears more lush and animate, greeting us similarly, carrying on its dynamic dance of energy. Our seemingly fixed, isolated body liberates and opens to something beyond its myopic self, uncovering a rich diversity of previously unavailable energy. It's common that Contacters finish

Unpredictable pathways: Robbie Kinter and Cheryl Pallant, (*below*) Frances Kimmel and Sharon Russell.

one seemingly exhausting dance and after refreshing with a few sips of water, adventure back onto the floor for the next dance.

In the very least, this newly made connection offers calm and relief. Depending on dancers' skill, awareness, and willingness, the exchange may also be transformative, uncanny, exhilarating, unnerving, blissful, exhausting. Many dancers, including those who have no formal affiliation with a particular religion, consider the dance spiritual. They are surprised that dancing, an experience that happens far from usual places of worship, affects them this way, yet calling the dance spiritual is not farfetched if we regard spirituality as connecting to an energy beyond our singular self, an experience independent of the dogma of any one religious institution. Contacter Lynn Stephens readily describes some of her dances as spiritual. "There are times when the boundaries between me and other melt and I begin to experience myself as part of a whole. CI is probably the way I experience that the most often. It's not me and another person, but something moving through us, and it surprises and delights me. It feels very deeply spiritual, more spiritual than anything I've experienced in a religious setting."[17]

The quality apparent here is crossing boundaries along with a heightened focus, what many religious traditions would characterize as mystical or spiritual. The experience transports ordinary perceptions into something more sensational, even ineffable. Divisive walls lower as the dance balances between effort and effortlessness, partners fully absorbed in themselves but also, paradoxically, each other. The constantly shifting combination of their bodies prompts expansion of perceptions and abilities beyond their usual range. Psychologist Mihaly Csikszentmihaly terms these experiences where self performs optimally and harmonizes with surroundings as "flow." "Contrary to expectation, 'flow' usually happens not during relaxing moments of leisure and entertainment, but rather when we are actively involved in a difficult enterprise, in a task that stretches our mental and physical abilities."[18]

Studying trance states which result from dance among indigenous people, anthropologist Holger Kalweit adopts a scientific perspective to explain such seemingly otherworldly phenomenon. For him, spirits and spirituality have more to do with the body's chemistry than anything mystical or numinous. "The spiritual experiences that have been venerated, cultivated, and fostered by these traditions are nothing more than a metabolic process, electrical stimulation at the organic molecular or cellular level.... Heightened stress, fear, panic, excessive effort, and physical overexertion stimulate endorphin production and trigger euphoric states."[19]

Certainly the rigor and spontaneous physical demands of the dance force each system to work at maximum capacity. Increased breath and the unpredictable, close proximity of a moving body demands keen alertness. This situation compares starkly with modern life with all its many conveniences where we may spend hour upon hour each week sitting in our car, at a desk, in front of the TV or computer, often alone, only our fingers in motion, busy pressing countless plastic buttons on a keyboard, the microwave, the ATM machine, the phone, CD player, and so forth. We are abundantly connected — technologically. Meanwhile the shin, elbow, underside of the thigh, and numerous other areas of the body fall idle and atrophy, contributing to an entire society largely disembodied, living primarily out of our heads, absorbed in thought, with few opportunities for direct, sensate connection. No wonder that a dancer awakens to a potential, spiritual or otherwise, residing no farther than a toe's reach away.

The reasons why Contacters perform the dance week after week, jam after jam vary among practitioners. Motivation comes from athletic, rigorous, relaxing, creative, meditative, exhilarating, instructive, nurturing, insightful, or healthy ideals. Individuals may use the dance for performance, to produce choreography, to develop bodily awareness, to keep fit, to refine perception, to navigate relationships, and to build community. Some Contacters don't need reasons beyond the fact that dancing is recreational and fun. Many individuals embrace CI precisely to be in touch, to feel inclusive in something larger than their solitary self. Although the route may be rocky at times, as dancers navigate the physical and psychological terrain of their moving relationship, the dance's intimate touch regularly yields genuine amity and connection.

A gift of CI, regardless of whether we stage our dance for an audience or keep it private in the studio, is that it reminds us not only that we *have* a body, but also that we *are* a body. And that body, though we may periodically prefer an updated model, is ultimately the vehicle for awakening to the world. Within the ongoing tug-of-war between what seems to be so and what probably is, between preferences and acceptances, the dance urges us most importantly to touch and be touched. In the process, we revive a more rudimentary and viscerally connected way of moving through space, the presence of another body reminding us of about our primal existence. In encountering the weight and mass of another, not only do we find home within the walls of our flesh, but we find, too, another similarly journeying.

QUESTIONS

- Which moods, if any, keep you from dancing? Are there any moods, like sadness or anger, that you consider inappropriate to being included in the dance? Do other dancers share the same standards?
- When someone stirs an emotion in you while you dance, how do you respond? Do you incorporate it into the dance, letting it evolve, or do you keep it apart?
- How often after a dance do you tell a partner about your experience? How often do you tell your partner what you valued about your dance? How often do you ask questions?
- What aspect of your dance with a partner is too risky to share in words? In what ways would sharing benefit the dance? In what ways might others be reluctant to mention something to you?

EXERCISES

The Spaces Between

Agree with a partner to slow the dance to a near halt periodically. Take turns saying "slow" as a cue. Aim to maintain a lively level of engagement while noticing how the dance changes. Find the balance between exerting effort and letting the dance assume its own direction without your willfulness. Notice shifts in balance and the compression of the contact point. Does the dance change heights? Are you more or less relaxed? Say "resume" to return your more natural momentum.

At other points in the dance, say "pause" and hold still in that position. Rest in place without allowing a lax attention. Allow breath to deepen, flesh to soften, tension to release. Focus on minute sensations, the rise and fall of your breath, your heat and sweat, the tightness or looseness of your clothes, the places where your body meets the floor and your partner. Focus, too, on the minute motions of your partner and whatever else captures your attention, the sound and feel of her breath, the strangeness or familiarity of her presence, the heat or cool of her skin, the texture of her clothes, the slick or matted surface of the floor, moments when comfort transitions in discomfort or rest into restlessness. Say "resume" to return to a more active dance.

Variation: Instead of slowing down, speed up.

Resonating

While dancing, imagine that your partner's every move is accompanied by sounds. Listen for them. A drone? Yelp? Purr? Buzz? Amplify them silently. Use them to provoke a gesture or quality of movement in yourself. Feel their pitch or rhythm resonating within. Use them to spur travel across the space while maintaining contact. Locate their vibration in a specific area of your body. Let the length or breadth of the sounds influence your stretches, rolls, twists, sprints, falls, and flights.

Begin to say them aloud. Both you and your partner respond to them in movement. Your partner can also respond in sound also.

Variation: As you dance, accompany your own movements with sound. Bark, groan, chirp, hum. Let your sounds be melodic or dissonant, quiet or loud, abrupt or smooth.

Variation: Both of you make your own sound simultaneously.

Phrasing

You and your partner write a list of phrases. Choose a category: Disruptions, Poetic Phrases, Scientific Truths, Architectural Features. Examples of Poetic Phrases may be "orbiting my family," "tumultuous arrival," or "submerged in a sea of roses." Include description in the phrase or an emphasis on action. Choose phrases because their meaning or sound appeals to you. As you and your partner dance, have someone read the phrases. Discover a way to incorporate the phrase into the dance. Have another phrase read and incorporate that one in.

Variation: Choose phrases randomly from books.

The Invisible Third

Without making contact, dance long enough for your movements to assume a distinctive quality. Approach someone else who is also soloing, but do not make contact. Keep this person in your peripheral awareness. Notice differences in your dances. Perhaps yours is floor-bound while the dancer nearby remains on her feet. Or her movements are small and intricate whereas yours are large and sweeping. Gradually find a way to make contact but also break the touch repeatedly. Notice the introduction of new movements and your difficulty or ease in maintaining your solo. Observe the intersections of moves, as well as the contrasts and complements.

Let your partner influence your solo. Imitate, enhance, amplify, and reverse her moves. Eventually let the contact and weight of your joining bodies take over. Instead of perceiving the dance as a You and a Me, two people engaged in separate trajectories of motion, look for a distinguishing Us, a third party that neither of you control. Consider that third party "gravity" and actively engage with it. Or consider it "impulse" or "flow."

Get to know this third party. Discover its current, its undertow, its gusts, its charge. Let the third party lead the dance, with you and your partner's occasional guidance. Let it guide the motion, the rests, and the rhythm. Resist it; play with it. Sense its influence upon your spine, your balance, your breath. Be sensation and responsiveness. Quiet thought. Be motion.

Partnering Metaphors

After a dance, you and your partner each choose a metaphor that describes your experience of the dance. For instance, if you choose fire, is it raging flames or a quiet flicker? Does the fire remain the same throughout the dance? You might choose one image for your-self, another for your partner, and yet another for the entire dance. Compare your metaphors. Discuss the ways your metaphors and your perceptions of the dance differ or show similarities.

Variation: Choose a metaphor first and then use it to generate a dance.

Moving Through Turbulence

Recall a difficult dance. Tell your partner about that dance. Recreate the dance, with your partner assuming your role. The recreation doesn't have to be exact. Perhaps choose to exaggerate the difficulty, include its opposite, or vary it in some way. Discuss how the new dance differs from the original one.

Switch roles. Let your partner tell you about a difficult dance and recreate that dance.

Variation: Do the same but choose an embarrassing or another emotionally charged dance.

Divination

You and your partner select a tarot card. Other divinatory tools like the I-Ching, the Bible, or the dictionary can also be used. Discuss the selections. Incorporate their qualities into the dance.

6

The Tribal Body:
Creating Community

*There is a simpler way to organize human endeavors. It
requires a new way of being in the world. It requires being
in the world without fear. Being in the world with play and
creativity. Seeking after what's possible. Being willing to
learn and to be surprised.*
— Margaret Wheatley and Myron Kellernan-Rogers

At the East Coast Contact Improvisation Jam in West Virginia
one year, I ventured away from the historic mansion to take a walk in
the woods. The solitude of the path and the cool air provided a reprieve
from the heat of constantly moving bodies. Recently fallen leaves
crunched underfoot and birds chirped and whistled, a musical inter-
lude interrupted by a small jeep bouncing along the stone rutted path.
I stepped aside to let the vehicle pass, but it stopped alongside me.

Eager to justify his appearance on private property, the driver
explained how friends had told him about the retreat center, Claymont
Court, and curiosity compelled him to finally check it out. He asked
a barrage of questions, but what puzzled him most were his findings
when he opened the mansion doors: "I knocked and knocked and no
one answered," he explained, "so I let myself in. There were dozens of
shoes near the door. I called again, but no one responded — what sort
of place is this?"

I supplied a short history of Claymont Court and introduced
myself as a participant with the current seminar. "I am of the People
of the Shoes," I said playfully before describing CI and some of the

activities of a typical extended jam. It is always a challenge to provide a concise definition, but I described CI as a modern improvisational dance which relies heavily on partners keeping a physical connection to one another as they share weight and roll, fall, spiral, leap, and slip along the contours and momentum of moving bodies. I explained how the dancers came from across the country, and some even from overseas, with the sole purpose of dancing together. Unfamiliar with modern dance, let alone CI, he expressed interest in what he perceived as "bacchanalian" activities and asked if he could join in. I invited him to the performance that evening and the open style dancing of a boogie that followed.

That night, once the music and dancing began, only a few performing CI, he wasted no time stationing himself near one woman, and then another, trying to win favors and steer their sexual attentions upon him. When his repeated advances proved fruitless, he quietly slipped out the door and did not return. It is no surprise that he left; his expectations failed to materialize, his preconceived image of the evening a far match from its reality. His directive agenda did not accord with the CI community he had entered, one whose etiquette draws from the dance itself and favors norms like mutuality over unilateral exchanges. The CI community welcomes newcomers, yet he did not recognize the behavioral norms of Contacters and chose to remove himself from the situation rather than look closer and find a way to fit in.

BEYOND COMMUNITY

I use the word community, aware that, for the most part, Contacters rarely share the common factor of geography, a typical way community is defined. *The American Heritage Dictionary* defines community foremost as "a group of people living in the same locality and under the same government."[1] Contacters live in many regions in numerous cities across many countries. They go to great lengths to gather, sometimes traveling long distances to gather weekly for a few hours, several days, or in some cases, a few weeks for an opportunity to dance. A minority in any given locale, those in one city or country consider those who reside elsewhere, even thousands of miles away, a member of the same community. What Contacters share is a common interest. The fellowship of the community is so strong and congenial that dancers often find instant community with their counterparts thousands of miles away. The common interest establishes a strong bond. It's common, for instance, for a dancer living in Boulder, Colorado, to travel to Berlin, Germany, phone a Contacter he never met before, and after a brief conversation, be offered a place to stay.

Common Language

The CI community is distinguished by its reliance on kinesthetics. Engagement with self, other, and the world depends heavily upon this language. Expression, communication, and understanding occurs through this channel, through movement, touch, and an interaction with space and mass. Obviously, CI is the central activity, which coincides with warm-ups, round-robins, and, occasionally, other related improvisational structures. Depending on the skills and interests of Contacters in a given locale, complementary activities such as Authentic Movement, free-form dancing, performance, yoga, and drumming may be included.

As creative participants in the mutable moment, the community gathers to dance within the intimate space of jointly moving bodies. Usually one or a few people assume the role of organizers whose prime purpose is to ensure that rent checks get paid and the space is suitable for jamming. They may focus on basics like making sure the heat is turned on and the floor kept clean. For longer jams, organizer's roles are more complex. Organizers typically establish a loose schedule of events and tend to the numerable details that come with bringing dozens of folks together, all in need of food and lodging. Some organizers lead dances; however, many leave the details to the dancers present. Such a laissez-faire approach has its benefits and shortcomings. On the one hand, it encourages all to be invested in planning as equal contributors. On the other hand, the time spent deciding, often by consensus, about, for instance, when or if to allow music to accompany a jam, is time not devoted to dancing.

SAFETY WITHIN THE COMMUNITY

From the moment dancers enter the jam space, safety becomes a primary concern. Because of the risks involved, the community agrees to make the space safe for investigations into the dance both physically and emotionally. To assist the community into transforming the flat surface of a wood dance floor into a welcoming space for engaging their moving bodies in concert with one another, all remove shoes and jewelry and dress in loose-fitting clothes like T-shirts and sweatpants. On the dance floor, verbal conversation falls away to increase peripheral and internal awareness. As dancers warm up, perhaps lying on their back or standing, all shift attention to respond more keenly to the murmur of cells and the rhythm of bodies.

The dance floor allows for the staging of many a drama, drawn from named and unnamed impulses, a mix of friction and momentum, the flux of bodies united in motion, carried out in complicity with spontaneity and play. One couple may focus on deepening breath through slow, careful stretches while another couple launches into a speedier, playful exchange with sprints and taunts at the perimeter of the floor. A newly discovered stretch of muscle, a sudden yelp, aggressiveness, volatility, tenderness, disorientation, spirals, elongations — these and more become the pattern and color on the dance floor.

Jams are open to a variety of expression, unlike a class in which a teacher directs students into specified movements and activities and everyone is expected to participate actively. Jams leave the quality and length of a dance to be determined by each dancer. One dancer may have a series of short dances or one long dance. A dancer may move on the dance floor for the entire time allotted to use the space, a soloist one moment, then part of a duet, then a trio, the particulars of the dance changing with each new combination. A dancer may have one brief dance before sitting out to watch the steady shuffling of partners or to talk quietly with a fellow Contacter. Depending on the energy of the group or any one dancer, the ambience of the room — or any one section — may erupt into a flurry of activity or settle into reflective steadiness.

IMPLIED NORMS

As with any community, members share a set of behavioral norms and values. None are explicitly stated. Instead, these principles derive from the very same ones practiced on the dance floor. Dancers focus primarily on three things: mobilizing the body, maximizing movement ability and responsiveness, and findings ways for the dance to emerge improvisationally in relationship with a partner, all done in an attitude of respect, trust, and support.

With CI a consensual form, dancers learn not to impose their

Spontaneous flight: Eric Ortega, Courtney Cooke, and Burr Johnson.

agenda upon another, or do so by always giving their partner an out. For instance, a dancer may want to lift a partner and get into position to do so. Some lifts require a firm hold on the partner. If the partner is unwilling to be lifted, shifting his center of gravity away from the lift as an indicator, the dancer initiating the movement needs to release his grip.

One rarely assumes the lead role through the entirety of a dance without consent. Typically, both partners control the pace and direction of the dance. For the most part, dancers look for common ground, the character and quality of the dance determined in its moment of unfolding. No one railroads another into an exchange that is inconsiderately one-sided, pushing a partner's desires and inclinations aside. Any sort of movement, from the outrageous to the subtle, can be introduced, yet no proposal comes with a guarantee of adoption into the dance for more than the few seconds it manifests. A dancer may jump repeatedly, urging the partner to join in. The partner may instead fall to the floor or slip below the jumper's arm to derail the motion. It's fine for dancers to introduce an idea or propose a movement before or during the dance, but they must also ascertain bodily cues to distinguish the difference between a green, red, or yellow light. The violation is committed in the attitude of the offering, the assumptions made, and the distractions entertained, particularly if they belittle, compromise, or ignore regard for partners. For example, some Contacters find such a thrill in spinning and flying a partner that they enthusiastically scoop up a partner and ignore the signs of reluctance or unwillingness. I've sometimes heard an emphatic "Stop!" or "Put me down!" in attempt to redirect the course of the dance to movements more mutually agreeable.

On the floor and off, Contacters often highly regard the perspective of others, generating dialog not monolog, cooperation not hostility, inclusivity not exclusivity. The respect granted toward oneself extends to all. Rather than feel threatened by a differing point of view, the community tries its best to support varied perspectives, investigating how and where an idea or activity can be adopted. Decisions concerning, for instance, lighting, a warm-up, or the introduction of a new score are frequently made by a group, not an individual. Not that individuals are prevented from asserting their unique interests and requests. Among some groups, a charismatic, convincing, or experienced dancer may regularly steer decisions while in other groups, problems and actions regularly are determined by group discussion and consensus. Generally, however, the group looks for ways to include a variety of perspectives, not only the dominant one.

Trust constitutes a basic tenet of the community. Off the dance floor, Contacters are likely to move quickly through social formalities to engage in substantive exchanges, conversations, stories, ideas, jokes, and feelings that may otherwise occur over a duration of time or be reserved for longtime friends. For the most part, the usual inhibitions and distrust apparent in the initial phase of interpersonal exchanges have already been displaced by the intimate actions on the floor. Despite a readiness to extend it, however, trust is not something that individuals blindly provide. Trust is not given wholesale simply because a dancer identifies himself as a Contacter; however, such identification typically means there are fewer barriers to overcome.

PRESUMPTIONS AND ADAPTABILITY

During the dance, assumptions can prove physically dangerous. It is unwise, for instance, to wield full weight onto partners without testing their strength and endurance. It can be similarly perilous to fly into a partner's arm simply because he or she *appears* large enough or strong enough. The hoped for catch may fail miserably because of the partner's inexperience or because the partner has already done so innumerable times in the last hour to the point of exhaustion. In both physical and verbal exchanges, assumptions must be continually measured against the stew of sensory phenomena available in each moment. Not to say that Contacters must be assured one hundred percent before attempting a move. To the contrary, CI encourages taking risks, moving beyond usual levels of comfort and seeming predictability to test uncertain waters. Give full weight. Land belly up. During lunch,

Risky heights: Dirk Spruck (*top*) and Roy Wood.

mention charged topics like politics or the annoying wart on your foot. The very act of constantly dipping into turbulence or calm, or mercurial or predictable circumstances, generates a firm foundation for building trust and the ability to discern the differences between a calculated risk and a foolish one, distinctions that a new and unskilled dancer learns through experience. Whether the outcome is friction or harmony, Contacters learn to be adaptable, to handle the unexpected, to let go when need be, to rise to any occasion, or to roll with a fall. For example, my pliancy is essential with my penchant for hanging upside down when in a trio. Often, in an exuberant bound, I flip my body upside down to land gleefully with ankles or knees hanging from my partners' shoulders or arms. Sometimes my partners catch my flinging body. Other times, they do not, and my balance and legs must compensate and find the floor without the assistance of my partners.

FORMING BONDS

The intimacy of the dance and the boundaries it crosses contributes to steadily building trust and enhanced communication. What is typically private, the particulars of our body, weight, smell and so forth — essentially the close proximity of our personal self — becomes the territory shared with another. The usual civilities of culture and efforts to conceal our physical selves in polite talk fall to the wayside in favor of the unmediated body. Interaction occurs on the primal level of being. Crawling, sweating, heaving, falling, stretching, pushing, and contracting bodies more viscerally engage in the pathos and poetry and fear and delight of physical existence. With one body close against another, the dance eclipses the more common mode of interaction which typically relies upon verbal communication and keeping a physical distance.

The potent combination of risk taking and the intimacy of the moving contact point exposes what in any other circumstance we may successfully conceal: raw vulnerability, hesitancy, discomfort, insecurity, awkwardness, confusion, apprehension. Like wayward schoolchildren, many of these untoward qualities poke their unkempt heads out in the dance, an exposure that can be as unnerving as it can be transformative. We fearfully grab a shoulder, a muscle contracts, our breath halts, we gasp or screech, we surprisingly fall to the floor. The attendance of these risks in the dance cultivates a deeper level of trust than is found in general daily encounters with colleagues, family, and friends; we often lean toward safe, predictable encounters that do not challenge abilities. By contrast, actions which shake up habits can awaken new abilities and help establish new connections. For example, lying belly up on a partner who is squatting on the floor, or worse, upright and in motion, leaves many dancers feeling vulnerable. We are accustomed to seeing the floor, and this position places the floor precariously out of view, our well-being out of our hands. Many of us prefer to be in control of our body at all times, yet the arch of our back limits the range of our movement and creates a dependence on our partner. When we resolve the position without injury, we have expanded the purview

131

of our body and learned, too, about the reliability of our partner. Risking such exposure on the floor without suffering negative consequences, Contacters may be emboldened to exhibit similar behavior socially, perhaps acting more spontaneously or speaking less circumspectly.

The bonding begun during the dance lays firm ground for what continues off the floor. A great dance with a partner does not ensure a great conversation at lunch nor a consequent harmonious relationship; but more realistically, new skills develop and various fears lose their potency, leaving increased self-confidence, a characteristic that aids in a variety of situations, not just with the one with whom we originally danced. In coming to know and expanding our contents, both the idiosyncratic and the common, we increase access to self which generates greater opportunity for genuine communication and connection.

The trust and confidence acquired in the process tie in to three qualities inherent in CI: authenticity, acceptance, and flow. A treasure of the dance is its opportunity to strip off the masks that society has us wear. Direct contact with heat, breath, and energy and their rises and falls loosens such masks or removes them altogether, prompted by a more acute sensitivity to our many subtle bodily cues. The dance intensifies awareness of phenomenon that many of us may have been conditioned to ignore, that may escape notice altogether, or that are considered unworthy. We begin to notice the slightest shift in respiration, the flash of an image, the surfacing of a memory, and heat pervading a muscle. At first, these events may seem unrelated to our current circumstances, yet they constitute the ebb and flow of Being in our moment of becoming. Such bodily phenomenon frequently gets overlooked in favor of the mental preoccupation of the day, or hour.

Aside from the time on the floor where the athletics of the dance demand a shift in attention, we dwell, for the most part, in our minds, not our bodies. Western thought situates the mind in the head, not the heart as do eastern cultures. Body-Mind Centering founder Bonnie Bainbridge Cohen goes even further, assigning mind, or awareness, to every cell in the body.[2] The mental prattle preoccupies us, sometimes serving as a welcome guide and companion. Other times it wields judgments, commentary, and instructions, a dictatorship neglecting the

Following impulses: Brandon Crouder and Corinne Mickler.

entirety of the body. Routine attention rarely has us attending to the whispers, the fluctuations of energy, the difficulty or ease in which we employ a muscle. Such attention may challenge preconceptions and reveal our underutilized and undeveloped bodily-kinesthetic intelligence, an idea similar to education theorist Howard Gardner's theory of multiple intelligences.[3]

Routinely, attention is directed away from the present moment where change is constant and visceral. A close look at the present moment reveals how boundaries and definition blur with every inhalation and exhalation. We may linger on the floor overlong across someone's back, unsure when or how the next move will occur. Will partners bolt upright back-to-back, or will they ooze into a new position from sharing weight? Such attention invites conscious participation in the unknown, the amazing dance of the unraveling moment. Sharing such raw awareness with another establishes common experiences and can lead to substantial relationships.

CHOICE AND AUTHENTICITY

The heightened attention requisite to the dance outlines differences between what is authentic and what is half-hearted, what gets backed with muscle and what gets aborted. The authentic is not confirmed to a narrow definition, however. What's genuine cannot be categorized as items only from column A. Likewise, the inauthentic cannot be quickly summed up in a single gesture, nor do sirens blare if someone lapses into fakery. Quite the opposite; there is much play in the recovery and revelation of untried, unfamiliar, *and* customary movements. What shines as genuine one moment may lose its shimmer in a consequent moment. Only whimsical footwork one moment and then an exacting handstand. A languid movement may indicate a block in energy. Though it may prompt a lull in the dance, sticking with it may be a worthwhile pursuit toward material that transforms into something more palpable, fluid, and clearly articulated.

Through play, a constant testing of boundaries, turning things

Truth revealed in presence: Eric Ortega and Burr Johnson.

around, inside out, and upside down, dancers respond to sensations and impulses, inviting what is familiar and conscious *and* what is foreign. Dancers learn to recognize their habituated patterns of movement and can clear channels for new or increased energy, expanding their movement repertoire in the process. Allowing play eliminates the usual tendency to judge, encourages poking and prodding, scampering and leaping, all the while increasing understanding and building skills. A dancer may attempt a handstand and then determine the fear too great and swiftly adopt a safer position. Approached in an attitude of play, the dancer can learn from the aborted movement. But if a dancer judges himself, shame or failure may push aside the experience from consideration altogether, the dancer learning nothing from the process.

Contacters practice acceptance of a great diversity of material, so rolling with whatever material makes its unruly or majestic appearance in the dance reinforces a continuous flow and embodied connection. At no time does a dancer have to turn off awareness of the body's events. With broad acceptance and going with flow, there are no failed moves, only a mind labeling the movements as such. Hips swinging side-to-side are just that, not flamboyance or confusion or any other judgment. An accepting attitude promotes a thorough rummage through the treasure chest, uncovering gems and ancient scrolls, as well as threadbare cloth and dust. Contacters are encouraged to clench fists, to roll into a tight ball, flop to the side, to push beyond or yield to their usual limits. As a result, movement expression arises at the cusp of consciousness and unconsciousness, drawing impartially from what is embedded in deep and unfamiliar recesses of flesh and from what grazes the surface. Spontaneous expression contains an edge, creative urge, and vitality often missing in a communication that is more controlled and familiar.

CREATING SPACE AND TOLERANCE

Many of these offhanded and unguarded traits show up in interpersonal exchanges within the community who demonstrates a great

A communal space for expression: (*clockwise from top*) Brad Stoller, Frances Kimmel, Sharon Russell, Kevin Heffernan, Jennifer Stanger, John Swift, and Page Ghaphery.

tolerance for diversity, eccentricity, risk-taking, opposition, and playfulness. Having already brought so much of themselves into the dance, the community is more likely off the floor to risk revealing parts of themselves ordinarily kept at bay. The community ushers forth finesse as well as less developed, even difficult or vulnerable qualities into the light. Contacter Karen Knight recalls attending her first jam, "All my feelings of inadequacy were coming out of every pore and I expressed them here [at the jam], and it was totally okay. I got a lot of support. I can play with them when it's uncomfortable because I know they're accepted. That's rare for me."[4]

The permissions granted by oneself extend more readily to others off the floor. Honoring the whole self, not just parts the culture or the individual deems worthy, sends a green light for others to do the same. Tolerance and support contribute to people becoming more capable of acknowledging the many shades of our humanity, from the foibles and griefs to the strengths and accomplishments. The group collectively is more willing to explore a variety of states of being and extend generosity. Curiosity, openness, and an investigative attitude replace fear, hostility, and the need for approval, these latter traits often guiding many social situations. Judgments, certainly not absent altogether, take a back seat to qualities like sympathy, adaptability, understanding, and resiliency. I've witnessed several instances when a dancer became angry or upset about a situation. Rather than flee the room or inflame the situation further through blame or incendiary comments, a group of dancers gathered around the distraught dancer to hear him out and together find a solution. For instance, one dancer shoved, lifted, and spun partners with little regard for their comfort or safety. Those dances, unsurprisingly, were brief. When his hostility showed no sign of abating, a group confronted him, and within the hour, his demeanor changed and he was back on the floor.

On the floor and off, acceptance, support, and welcoming what's hidden or latent into the open encourages growth and connection. The unconscious takes form, finds a place, a voice, a gesture. Once seen, it may linger in the newly found light, disappear, or transform into something else. Whatever its fate, by familiarizing ourselves with our contents, it is easier to inhabit ourselves, to welcome deep, resonant breath, to tap into our vast resources, and consequently engage similarly with another, be it while sharing dinner, conversation, or a dance.

It's no surprise that principles from the dance influence community members, lives. CI is an activity that reinforces embodiment, and the lessons and understandings garnered on the floor become difficult to shut away, to dismiss solely as dance-specific skills with no further application. The dance alters biology, unravels patterns, and releases habitual tensions. The body is the medium of the art; dancers cannot close the door and leave their work behind them in the studio. Although some dancers do compartmentalize the dance and keep it separate from life beyond the floor, for others, the physical changes and insights gleaned during practice of the craft walk out the door with them. Says veteran Contacter Steven Harris, "We figure out new ways to hold our body and new ways to move through the world. We're not restricted to certain movements. We've found our body and change ourselves because of it."[5]

CI becomes practice for what is possible as a body, initially manifesting as a rich dance on the floor, much of which spills gladly into other areas of life. The majority of Contacters are not professional dancers; they refine their embodiment skills not for the stage, but for jamming. But the skills also influence their lives off the dance floor, perhaps manifesting in their occupations. For Contacter Joe Tranquillo, a biomedical engineer, lessons of CI resurfaced at his office. While at a jam, a fellow dancer had pointed out that he relied too much on his muscles during lifting and recommended that if he let the momentum of the dance determine when and how to raise someone up, he would find it easier. Tranquillo drew a parallel to his approach at the office. "I'll be sitting at my desk, saying I need to get this done, yet nothing is getting done. Now I ask if there's something else I can do, and usually there is. I go with the flow and come back to what I need to do, and I'm much more productive and happy in the long run."[6] Learning from the dance, Tranquillo abandoned his enslavement toward constant goal setting for a more flexible and fluid approach and found great benefit in doing so. Contacter Susan Singer experienced a similar analogy between her dance and her life, carrying the dance into her family life. The mother of three, she relates, "I get to play with my kids. I wrestle with them, bump into them on purpose. I'm not so uptight and trying to control everything as I used to."[7]

As the dancing body moves toward increasing its range, building skills, creatively negotiating space and mass, nerves find new connections, perceptions refine, and our many parts integrate into a more adaptable whole, uncovering options where before few or none existed. The dance functions as a laboratory for what's possible as a living organism actively participating in its becoming, an evolution that is as much a solitary experience as a shared one.

Dance Mirroring Life

Contacters regularly find analogies between the particulars of their dance and how they move through the day and structure their lives. Some find that the dance illuminates their daily habits. Long-time Contacter and jam organizer Cynthia Carter-Rounds, who passed away in 2006, recognized the correlation between how she maneuvers on the floor and off: "I did in my dances what I did in my relationships."[8] Never lifting the dance off the floor may suggest an unwillingness to take risks or a fear of standing up to challenges. Dances regularly performed at high speeds that lead to injury may suggest a reluctance to attend to details. Although it's up to the interests of each dancer to explore the correlation, like dream analysis, there is no simple translation in their lives.

For many Contacters, the interactions on the floor raise pivotal questions about how they conduct their lives and point out the possibility for change. Recognizing patterns in their movements and behaviors leads dancers to question and investigate options. Repeatedly I hear from my students about changes in their relationships with coworkers, family, even casual strangers. CI, like many other physical practices, reduces stress which heightens receptivity to the moment. But CI also highlights how we move and interact, when we react, and points out previously unseen options. So many athletes praise the physical benefits of CI that what started as a trickle of athletes in my university CI classes has led to my teaching an entire university basketball team and, recently, more and more soccer players. In unique cases, the lessons of CI are applied to community living — literally. Interested in exploring CI principles in relation to daily conduct and mundane chores, CI teacher Carolyn Stuart offers month-long workshop intensives. Building on the principles of greater personal responsibility and mutual respect, ideals drawn from the dance, workshop participants not only improvise together on the dance floor, but look for new ways to live together and carry out chores. After a two-month intensive, she found, "It became clear that this way of being together was very unusual and very challenging to stay with. The habits of assuming and accusing are strong, as is the need to establish power over others in order to determine a sense of self worth or control."[9]

CREATIVE ENGAGEMENT

In a world increasingly geared toward doing and accomplishing, there are few communal spaces for summoning and dancing our creative, emergent self. Where else can we abandon our addiction to materialism or obsession with achievement to participate instead in an activity rooted in our inherent biology that opens to the vast wilderness of Being, beyond the paved road and satellite dish? Where else do we get to dance with the complexity of our cells and give them their full due? Where else do we listen to the music of our bodies, participating in a improvisatory and vitalizing physical dialog that questions limitations and urges embodiment? Where else do we get to explore and practice, trusting the mystery of our bodies in intimate partnership alongside others on the same journey?

The demands and challenges of the dance set the CI community apart from others who are either uninterested or too fearful to ever take the initial step onto the floor. This shared, heartfelt, body-felt experience generates profound affinities within the community who has developed a specialized language and norms. Though innumerable traits can distinguish a community, for psychiatrist and minister M. Scott Peck, Contacters epitomize his definition of community, due to one notable quality — the ability to genuinely communicate with one another. He says,

> In our culture of rugged individualism — in which we generally feel that we dare not be honest about ourselves, even with the person in the pew next to us — we bandy around the word "community." We apply it to almost any collection of individuals — a town, a church, a synagogue, a fraternal organization, an apartment complex, a professional association — regardless of how poorly these individuals communicate with each other. It is a false use of the word. If we are going to use the word meaningfully we must restrict it to a group of individuals who have learned how to communicate honestly with each other, whose relationships go deeper than their masks of composure, and who have developed some significant commitment to "rejoice together, mourn together," and to "delight in each other, make others' conditions our own."[10]

It is difficult for a dancing body to lie. Truth manifests everywhere, in the way we hunch our shoulders, in the way we consistently yield to another's weight, in the way we encounter the floor. The dance sweeps away pretense, unfolding new ways to greet the challenges of our environment and those who populate it. It is the type of activity that art critic Suzi Gablik encourages. Once an advocate of modernist art which she explains as pitting individuals against society, Gablik calls for art that respects participation and connection. She explains, "Most of us, in the capitalist world, have never had an experience of true community. We live so much in an ethos of professionalism, which keeps us bound to individualistic modes of thought and directed toward the marketing of products, that it is difficult not to marginalize, or subtly discount, achievements that manifest less ego–control, and point to the value of cocreativity."[11]

The CI community embraces collaborative creativity. Together dancers find a way to connect with the floor, their first partner, welcoming the consequent unpredictability and vulnerability of moving

Connecting outward and within: Page Ghaphery, Brad Stoller and Frances Kimmel.

bodies in contact with one another. For many, entering the skin of this community is not easy. The values and behaviors of Contacters, who place great emphasis on proprioception and kinesthetic activities, differ markedly from those of western society, where involvement with the world is much less tactile and much more isolated.

HISTORICAL CHANGES

Ours is a society that largely promotes a numbing immobility which, if we're not careful, slowly dulls us into lethargy. We are far from our agrarian past which situated bodies in fields, feet in touch with the earth, hands wrapped around tools, bodies muscling with the toil of cultivating crops. From the industrial age onward, rapid technological growth has replaced physical labor with machines and computers. Intending to relieve the body of backbreaking labor and hasten production, these new technologies have a downside; reinforcing disembodiment by limiting or eliminating entirely any contact with the physical world. Whether applied to work or leisure, labor saving devices and conveniences like remote controls, voice-generated dialers, automatic garage door openers, and lawn mowers simplify the daily grind, yet at the same time they reduce opportunities for tactile engagement with the world. Regardless of our job, the many chores we carry out daily, or any of the particulars that occur from the moment our head lifts off the pillow to the moment it returns, if we do not intentionally engage the body as an alert, investigative, sensual vehicle, we are all susceptible to the debilitating consequences of habituation.

Although in recent years yoga has been widely embraced, and America's fondness for jogging continues unabated, mainstream society, for the most part, provides few avenues to explore the creative body in motion and in relationship with others. Walking, once a mainstay for getting around and meeting neighbors, is steadily threatened by a proliferation of roads without sidewalks. Our popular methods of transportation, cars and airplanes, keep us passive, moving us at super speeds while our bodies remain motionless, strapped into a seat where we press a pedal (if not using cruise control), turn a steering wheel, or lift a cell phone. No wonder there's such interest in extreme sports like bungee jumping which, for a few intense seconds, floods our otherwise lax body with sensation.

We've gone so far in the race toward achieving the so-called good life that we overlook what gets left behind, the practice of connecting with others and living side-by-side in a way that promotes true community, not a happenstance of common geography. The modern lifestyle encourages more and more people to retreat into their separate lives, into their separate vehicles and separate homes, where each family member is rewarded with his own room, television, computer, telephone, and so forth — enviable signs of status. Little consideration is given to the isolation created by such ownership. Outside the home, the town center, once an area for varied commerce and casual meetings, is increasingly rendered economically defunct due to suburban sprawl. Local politicians and developers constantly threaten to construct buildings on common spaces like city parks and other open spaces in order to generate a tax base and profit. Movie multiplexes and computer games have become some of the most popular forms of entertainment, not community centers or cafes where groups can meet and be the directors of their own attention. CI aims to overcome this and recreate community.

CI is an activity that supplies inroads to our body while simultaneously revealing areas of intersection with others. A Contact jam displays the motion of individual bodies while divulging, too, the routes and rhythms for interaction. A jam offers an opportunity to develop and express our kinesthetic self and learn ways to substantively engage with others, a creative and collective honoring of both individuals and a group. As a communal activity, Contacters reclaim themselves, finding a home within, while discovering suitable fits with others. The degree of cooperation shows an inherent desire for compatibility, gratifying a need for comradery that leaves no one behind. With the dance as the center of attention, no one's ego is privileged above others, everyone's idiosyncrasies of personality and movement encouraged to find a place within the dance. The dance holds center stage, and participants look for ways to enter the fray, either on the floor or along its edges.

It's worth remembering the origins of dance as an inseparable thread in the fabric of society. Dance once regularly marked key events like planting crops, initiating a hunt, going to war, marrying, announcing a birth, or preparing for death. Dance was used to help communities cope with transitions from one stage of life to another. Dance brought a community out of its separate dwellings and concerns to reveal a part of its humanity otherwise hidden by the busyness of daily life. It functioned, to use anthropologist Victor Turner's phrase, as "a hall of mirrors" in which all could see themselves and modify behavior.[12] The activity summoned all to acknowledge both the mundane and the sublime. With early dance allied with ritual and theater, often providing a cathartic and integrative role, dancers and viewers alike recognized its importance. The dance, working with ills, joys, and conflicts, helped a community see itself and renew commitments to its values. Body, earth, self and other were integral, a union that allowed no division.

With support for dance hard to come by in recent decades, professional dancers face great financial challenges in securing rehearsal space and performing. There is no sign that the situation is getting easier. Social critic Camille Paglia notes how television and radio are increasingly derisive toward the arts, dance being the most fragile in that "it cannot flourish in isolation or with long fallow periods."[13] As for future generations, SOL-driven public schools, emphasize subjects like math, history, science and English and offer no dance classes — unless on the rare occasion a teacher volunteers for an extra-curricular after-school program. The result is that fewer people are regularly exposed to dance and are educated to understand its value, contributing to a climate in which creatively engaged bodies get dismissed, misconstrued, or disparaged.

Contacters find coming home to their bodies empowering and transformative. In fully surrendering bodily to the dance, yielding the truth of our being to the physics of a partnered dance, we end up healing fissures in a world otherwise compartmentalized and bound. In opening the gates to our potential, reflexes heighten, awareness awakens, and habits are pushed from bed to greet the birth of each moment.

In many ways, the practice of CI is simple. Collect a few like-minded, willing people, make physical contact with a partner and follow each other's contours and momentum. Participate in the laws of gravity. Discover the native intelligence of the body. Easy. Yet because we typically abide by so many self-imposed and culturally-imposed limitations and few of us ever receive a movement education, we sever flow and cut off the natural roll or lift, trying to manipulate and control energy rather than abide by its currents. With CI, there is no goal, no failures, no wrong moves. Just this moment unfolding. Just this body listening and being listened to. A reciprocal exchange that regularly reinvents itself. Ordinary. But because attending to our original nature occurs so infrequently, we have lost that vital connection and an activity like CI gets cast as extraordinary.

LOOKING AHEAD

When Steve Paxton introduced CI to a handful of dancers in the '70s, he had little indication that it would take off to the degree it has. Not following in the tradition of modern dance predecessors who founded a company based on their particular style, he led CI's development by default, giving direction and encouragement when necessary but, for the most part, letting practitioners determine much of its direction themselves. As a result, some practitioners use CI to inform their choreography; couples may share their centers of balance and weight and uncover new ways they can lift, lean, and roll; individuals may stumble upon a new repertoire of movements. Many more CI practitioners are jammers primarily, with little or no interest in staging their movements. They attend jams regularly, enjoying the intensity of the dance and the close connections they establish with others. They may also carry the dance into other areas, such as their jobs and families.

The depth and speed with which Contacters connect with others find few parallels in other activities. Although the dance may send some scurrying to the nearest exit, for others, participating in CI is an invitation to reconnect with their lost selves, to establish a fundamental dialog, to remember and practice kinship, and to ride the contours and currents of their bodies. For an increasing number of dancers across the globe, these opportunities keep them returning again and again.

As a devoted practitioner, jam organizer, and Contact teacher, I have brought many CI principles into my poetry, into how I walk down the street, and into how I engage with strangers and friends alike. I sometimes wonder what my town would look like if more CI principles were set into motion. Instead of an upsurge in road rage, would we have road waves, drivers nodding acknowledgments to each other as their cars gracefully move in and out of lanes? Instead of peering out the window suspiciously at the strangers walking past our door, would we instead step out on the porch to greet them?

At the end of every CI class I've taught and during closing circles of weeklong jams, not one but several participants express reluctance in leaving and severing the bonds they have formed. Someone inevitably shares information about an upcoming class or jam as others scribble the information into notebooks, already considering how to rearrange their schedules to accommodate the event. Although all return to their separate lives, I have seen that the impact of the bonds generated while moving in close proximity continues. We may return to our homes, but the connections established on the floor live on in our bodies, settling in slowly and tangibly.

QUESTIONS

- How do you speak up in a community?
- How do you listen to another's point of view?
- How do you handle criticism? Develop a new way.
- How does your jam handle conflict? Discuss what to do theoretically. What is the easiest way to hear about a conflict?
- How can your jam benefit from the difficulties of one of the dancers? How is that person a beneficial teacher?

- Who are the dancers that typically support you? Offer support to the ones that typically ignore you.

- Who threatens you? In what way do they do so? In what ways might you threaten them?

- In what ways do you honor every member of your jam? How does each one make a valuable contribution?

- Have everyone if your jam respond to "Wouldn't it be nice if..." as relates to the jam.

- What do you value about your jam? In what ways could you make it better?

EXERCISES

Round Robin

This is classic CI. The entire group forms a circle. Two people, person "A" and "B," enter the circle and begin dancing. After several minutes, "C" joins the duet to form a trio briefly before replacing "A," who joins the rest of the group who are sitting out and awaiting a turn to dance. Continue rotating through dancers. The size of the group determines how many couples dance at any given time and how long each of the duets lasts.

Archetypes

Randomly assign archetypes to everyone in the group. Possibilities include The Troublemaker, The Flamboyant One, The Hesitator, The Savior, The Airy One. Come up with others. Write down the archetypes on slips of paper and randomly distribute them, without sharing who has been assigned which archetype. Embody the archetype while dancing with your partner. Rotate partners frequently, but keep the same archetype. Discuss later how these assignments influenced the dance.

Variation: Everyone gets a slip of paper, but many are left blank. Only a few dancers receive an archetype.

Global Partnering

Travel through the space while doing a solo dance. Orbit everyone. Consider everyone your partner, but do not make physical contact with them. Partner by either dancing across the room from them or in their vicinity. Place them in your focus without intending to influence them. Let your body respond to theirs. Mirror their rhythm, a stretch, a chosen part of the body, their tone, an energy. Alter the quality of your movement so it becomes something distinctively different from the original. Make it your own.

Clustering

After individually warming up, move through space until you find a partner. Have a short dance, no more than a few minutes. Separate and continue your solo dance until you find a new partner. Repeat the cycle with an aim to dance with everyone.

Let duets evolve into trios, quartets, quintets, forming clusters of dancers. Develop these dances so that each group develops its own identity. Have these groups meet up with another group, and let the dance evolve into yet another identity. Eventually bring all clusters together so that the entire group is dancing with an awareness of the whole.

7

The Dancing Body:
A Teacher's Sampler

This chapter is devoted to Contact Improvisation lessons to assist readers in furthering their exploration of the form and getting acquainted with a diversity of teachers and their styles. The lessons in the following pages offer a glimpse into what takes place in a teacher's class. Contacters quickly learn from attending classes that every teacher approaches the material differently. The outcome may be similar — guiding practitioners to embody themselves and encourage improvised movement unfolding from an ever-changing point of contact with a partner — but a teacher's method, deriving from training and personality, conveys a specialized awareness of the body. Some teachers rely on demonstrating an exercise and, with a minimum of words, getting participants to replicate the movements. Some teachers rely on studying anatomy by using both hands-on exercises and printed illustrations that expose the layers of the body under the skin, all of which explain the mechanics of the body and what contributes to moving effectively. Some teachers emphasize skills like rolling and sloughing; some stress guiding participants into a state of awareness to heighten perception and reflexivity; others carefully choose metaphors to match the power of imagination with the body's ability to manifest those images physically. All demonstrate a correlation between understanding the body on a multiplicity of levels and stirring it into motion.

Whatever combination of approaches teachers use, their style reveals itself in their choice of words, the details outlined in the steps, even the pacing of the exercise. Because CI is an improvisational dance unaffiliated with any institution, a CI teacher has great leeway in selecting material that best communicates entry into the moving body.

The lessons that follow come from a variety of teachers, primarily from the United States. Every exercise is written in the teacher's own words to preserve and reflect his or her individual styles. There are several warm-ups, essential precursors to the dance: Steve Paxton's historic "Small Dance" and Nancy Stark Smith's equally well-known "Shakedown." Exercises from Robin Gilmore, Alicia Grayson, and Eszter Gál introduce motion and awareness that aim at physical alignment and integration. Martin Keogh ventures into the territory of falling and befriending the floor. Brad Stoller, Jayne Bernasconi, and Kristin Horrigan all focus on skills with weight, its complement, gravity, and their relationship to flying. Brenton Cheng touches on the subject of saying no as a necessity for maintaining boundaries. Conversely, Carolyn Stuart challenges boundaries by presenting a koan exercise that breaks through mental and physical limits. Together, these lessons show the range of material contributing to Contact Improvisation, preparing you for attending a class and a jam.

SMALL DANCE

Steve Paxton

When founder Steve Paxton was developing the movements that came to be associated with Contact Improvisation, one of his explorations centered on the difference between rapid, frenetic motion and stillness. He believed stillness is never completely void of movement. Focusing attention on stillness reveals the minute, natural motion of the body. In "Small Dance," a signature warm-up, he guides us into attending to the micro-movements of the body that accompany standing as a way to uncover our primal sources of motion and to make them more readily apparent. The exercise encourages us to set aside the controlling mind and give in to the natural forces of the body necessary for dancing to unfold effortlessly.

Steve Paxton is the founder of Contact Improvisation. He is one of the founders of the Judson Dance Theater, Grand Union, and Touchdown Dance, a company for the visually disabled. He lives on a farm in Vermont and lectures, performs, choreographs, and teaches in the United States and Europe.

All you have to do is stand up and then relax and at a certain point you realize that you've relaxed everything that you can relax but you're still standing, and in that standing is quite a lot of minute movement ... the skeleton holding you upright even though you're mentally relaxing. Now, in that very fact of you ordering yourself to relax and yet continuing to stand —finding that limit to which you could no further relax without falling down — you're put in touch with a basic sustaining effort that goes on constantly in the body, that you don't have to be aware of. It's background movement static that you blot out with more interesting activities, yet it's always there sustaining you. We're trying to get in touch with these kinds of primal forces in the body and make them readily apparent. Call it the "Small Dance," a name chosen largely because it's quite descriptive of the situation and because while you're doing the stand and feeling the "Small Dance" you're aware that you're not doing it, so, in a way, you're watching yourself perform, watching your body perform its function. Your mind is not figuring anything out and not searching for any answers or being used as an active instrument but is being used as a lens to focus on certain perceptions.

SHAKEDOWN (EXCERPT)

Nancy Stark Smith

Since the earliest days of Contact Improvisation, Nancy Stark Smith has played a central role in the development of the dance. As part of her ongoing exploration into the relationship between the body and mind and as a preparation for dancing, she created the warm-up "Shakedown" to deepen kinesthetic experience and relax the body. She teaches the exercise in her Underscore, a dance structure designed to aid the teaching and practicing of CI. Much of CI relies on one often overlooked yet constant partner, the floor. Her exercises get us to feeling our weight with this partner. When we go through the exercise thoroughly, the floor transforms from a hard surface into a soft, reliable support and our perceptions more keenly detect various sensations.

Nancy Stark Smith travels the world teaching and performing CI and other improvised forms. She is the founding editor of Contact Quarterly, *which she continues to edit, and lives in Massachusetts.*

Begin lying on your back, releasing your weight to the floor and the earth below it. "Let gravity have you," as Steve Paxton says. Let the envelope of your skin enlarge to allow your contents to be under less pressure, to expand, breathe, settle. Feel the sensation of release as the tissue softens. Fall, fall, backwards to the center of the earth. Relax. Let the earth support you.

Notice the surfaces of your body that are touching the floor and let them soften, widen, and blend with the mass under you. "Read" what you're in contact with — sense through touch the floor's temperature, texture, stability, mobility. If you were lying on the deck of a boat in the water, it would feel very different.

Take a moment to consider the earth: its mass, size, and shape; its center underneath you — way, way down. Now consider *your* mass: your exact shape and size, density, center. Feel the affinity between these two masses, their attraction and relationship. Feel the big earth under you, easily supporting your weight. The weight you release into the earth comes back to you, in equal measure, as support.

As you continue to relax, let a little spark of energy come in through the tips of your toes. With that spark, activate the mass of the toes, wiggling them, mixing their mass with air and energy. Let the movement sweep around under the skin, mobilizing and refreshing the inside of the toes.

From the toes, open the channels through the joints into the mass of the feet, and gently activate their mass. Allow the movement to gather its own internal momentum, the mass mixing with air, the air moving through the mass. Fluff up the mass of the feet like a down comforter whose feathers have become matted. Separate the clumps of mass with this swirling movement, letting them unglue and break into little particles. The mass creates and rides the movement.

When satisfied, slide your focus from the feet up into the ankle joint and let movement arise there, shaking loose the mass, washing the inside of the joint with movement, soothing and stimulating as you go.

From the ankle, shift your focus into the lower leg ... knee joints ... thighs — mobilizing the mass, shaking it loose, opening paths of circulation by running movement streams around and through the tissue. Try different intensities, rhythms, and speeds to engage the mass.

Continue the passage of the swirling, shaking movement up through the body — from thighs into hip joints, and, gently, into the pelvis.... Mobilize, agitate, fluff the mass, cleaning out the dusty corners, fresh air blowing through. Let your exhalations carry out of the body whatever you don't need; let fresh air in.

Shift focus from pelvis into waist/navel area. A little activation gets it going. Notice how the mass, mind, mechanics, and movement here feel different from the mass of the pelvis. What's different? Relax, do what you can. Don't work too hard.

From the waist, open channels into rib cage, lungs, chest, top of the lungs, under armpits, the area where the rib cage tapers to the neck and throat. Shed light on dark corners, and welcome a breeze into unused areas. Remember to keep the chest relaxed and available for deep breaths to come, letting fresh air and nourishment into cells, exhaling old air.

From the top of the neck, let movement come up into the base of the head, streams of air circulating through the mass, lightening, mobilizing the head. Travel up through the southern hemisphere of the head to the equator (including inside the ears) and on to the northern hemisphere, tapering toward the crown of the head. When ready, let the activating force pass out of the body through the top of the head. Follow it mentally and see it dissolve in the space, feeling the movement in your body diminish, eventually coming to rest. Breathe easily, rest, and notice after-images and sensations.

The Shakedown can be done lightly, vigorously, swiftly, or at length. It can travel from head to toe or focus only on a specific part of the body, especially if an area feels dull or stuck. When the focus shifts from one area to the next, the previous area's activity subsides. It isn't an accumulation but a sequential pass through the body. Relax, engage, and enjoy the ride.

DEVELOPMENTAL MOVEMENT WARM-UP
Robin Gilmore

With her background as a bodyworker and performer, Robin Gilmore's warm-up reflects her ongoing interest in getting the body to move and function from an optimal state of integration and alignment. Achieving physical balance is pivotal to bearing weight in Contact Improvisation and allowing movements to arise from the body without undue strain. The body often has to be trained to move from a place without stress, and the exercise below provides a foundation for doing so.

Robin Gilmore first encountered CI in 1980. The form has long enriched her work as a dancer and somatic educator. Robin teaches the Alexander Technique and is the author of What Every Dancer Needs to Know About the Body.

In 1981 I was introduced to both Contact Improvisation and Release Technique at the Vermont Movement Workshop. The faculty included Marsha Paludan, Nina Martin, Danny Lepkoff, the late Nancy Topf and John Rolland. Developmental movement was a key part of Paludan's classes, and the sequence below is largely hers. Over the years, my relation to this material deepened as I subsequently became an Alexander Technique teacher. Developmental movement shows us how we came to walk upright on two feet, and it helps with ease and facility of movement and increases sensory awareness. All of these qualities support the practice and wonder of Contact Improvisation.

Before moving through the structured developmental sequence, you'll need to spend some time in stillness and gradually transition to amorphous spinal movement, yawning, sighing and rolling — lots of rolling. Rolling can be initiated from any number of body parts or images, and it's worthwhile exploring the whole gamut. You'll find pathways that are as comfortable as old pajamas as well as some mind-benders that feel alien or even frustrating. Expanding your movement affinities on the floor will open up your dancing when you're off the ground and in the air.

Now to the sequence.

Wriggling

On your back with knees bent toward your chest, initiate a tail wag from side to side, like a dog vigorously scratching his back. Movement travels up the spine so that your head also moves.

156

Child's Pose/Head-to-Tail Rocking

Roll into a ball so that your weight is on your shins with your forehead resting on floor and your sitting bones on heels. Arms are overhead on the floor at 90-degree angles. Feel the movement of your breath into your back.

Give gentle pressure through the tops of your feet to initiate a ripple from tail to head so that the top of your skull now rests on floor. To reverse, initiate by rolling your head towards your eyebrows as the tail reaches back to heels.

Creeping

Rise to forearms and knees with your spine parallel to floor. Think of letting your head lead through space as you wag your tail to propel you forward. This stage is low to the ground and self contained. It's useful to become familiar with this intermediate support place with weight on your entire forearm.

Crawling

Rise to your hands and knees. Let your head lead into crawling. Play with outer motivation such as sights and sounds. Crawl forward and backward. Chase your tail or someone else's.

Walking on Hands and Feet (Bear Walk)

From crawling, push back with your hands as your tail reaches up toward the ceiling. With weight distributed evenly on hands and feet, knees slightly bent, release your neck so that you're seeing the world upside down. Locomote in any direction, sort of a galumphing stride.

Crouch/Squat

Walk hands toward feet while bending your knees into full flexion. Your head rises as your tail reaches down toward your heels. If you cannot press your heels down to the floor, use your hands for balance and aim for ease in your neck and a long spine.

Standing

From the squat, let your head lead to standing. As an intermediary step, you may first return to the upside-down bear. Shift all the weight to your feet and roll up through the spine.Once you're familiar with the sequence, you can reverse it from standing and then move through all the stages, omitting the locomoting and increasing speed. Try it while sharing weight with a partner. The developmental sequence provides safe and reliable pathways in and out of the floor. From this foundation, your dancing can soar in any direction.

INCREASING AWARENESS OF THE SPINE

Alicia Grayson

The spine, comprised of 26 vertebrae and cushioned discs in between, is the central axis of the nervous system. Housing thousands of nerves and the corridor for spinal fluid and chi, the spine is an indicator of tension. A flexible spine is one that supports sensation, awareness of the body and its environment, and achieves the largest degree of motion. A way to attain flexibility is through applying pressure and carrying out undulating motions. To help us move more fluidly and recognize our organismic self, Alicia Grayson has us imagine ourselves as creatures who thrive in water and rely on easy, serpentine motion to get around. Introducing a range of motion to the spine, however small, is one of the quickest ways to heat the body and heighten awareness.

Alicia Grayson has taught CI and performed at universities, jams, and workshops in North America and abroad. Her teaching is influenced by nearly two decades of yoga and practices of meditation, Pilates, Body-Mind Centering and Authentic Movement.

Spinal warm-up on your own. Imagine being a creature that moves very fluidly, a snake, a fish, a sea otter in ocean waves. Play with head and tail leading, ends of spine moving apart and coming together, spine spiraling, coiling. Be aware of the volume of the spine, its front, back and sides. Feel the spine moving on the breath like seaweed in ocean waves.

Spinal warm-up with partner. Partner places hands on spine as both people continue to move from spine. The partner can place hands on front and back of spine as well as on top of head and sacrum or tail. Sense spine as the central channel of life force from which all other movement originates. Switch roles.

Solo moving into and out of the floor. Sense tail releasing to the earth as body rises up, head staying open to the sky as body falls to the earth.

Hands on partner's spine as tactile assist in rising and falling. As mover releases to floor, partner slides hand up spine from back of waist to top of head, assisting partner in keeping a sense of lightness. As mover rises out of floor, partner slides hand down spine from lower back to sacrum and down the legs to maintain a sense of grounding.

Solo moving from spine with the image of eyes in your scapula. Play with rising and falling, jumping and spiraling, imagining your partner's hands on your spine as a support for feeling this vital movement. Play with the space and other's movements like currents in the ocean washing through your back.

Continue to move as above with a partner but without physical contact in this back space/spinal dance. Allow the body to be a tease for physical contact.

Partners sitting back-to-back with legs stretched out. Sense each other's breath. One person releases to floor perpendicular to partner as top person releases through back, lying over partner. Maintain head/tail awareness. Experiment with pathways down and then return to sitting back-to-back.

Squatting back-to-back. One person releases to hands and knees. Support person maintains a strong head/tail awareness, imagining that head and tail lengthen infinitely away from one another. Top person slides pelvis over support person's pelvis and opens into the backspace with arms overhead. Enjoy the vastness of the space that opens above and around you as you catch the ride. Switch roles playing with the fluid transition of being under and over. Allow yourself to experiment and play with this mid-level back space partnering.

Standing back-to-back. Support person releases pelvis below partner's pelvis to offer a ride, extending tail away from top of head. As top person catches the ride, enjoy opening to the space above and around you. Play with fluid transitions of offering and receiving rides through the back space.

Moving back-to-back. Supporter gives an offer by shifting pelvis and head perpendicular to partner, not using the arms but only the spine for support. Top person releases back into partner; arms can stretch overhead as landing gear. Allow this to open up into a dance playing with your spine and back space. Let go of having to lift or take rides, stay with the enjoyment of moving with your own and partner's bodies.

A CLASS ON THE BACK

Eszter Gál

The sense we rely on predominantly is sight. Sight helps us position objects in space and aids us in establishing a spatial relationship with them. When trying to develop proprioceptive and kinesthetic awareness, our reliance on our eyes can impede sensing the more subtle cues that come with tactile exchanges. Eszter Gál asks us to close our eyes to focus and uncover the sensations elicited when we press ourselves back-to-back against a partner, the back being a wide, safe surface for initiating a contact point. The back-to-back connection contributes to building a solid relationship with a partner while preparing us to let the dance evolve into a wide variety of constantly changing contact points.

Eszter Gál is a dancer, teacher, choreographer, and member of L1 Independent Dancers Partnership in Budapest. Since 1993 she has been creating her choreographed and improvised works, collaborating with various artists in the field of music, dance and visual arts. She regularly teaches, leads and participates in international performance projects and festivals in Europe, Russia and the USA.

Focus on the entire back surface from base of the skull to tip of the shoulders to the pelvic floor.

First Step

Begin with partners sitting back-to-back. The touch is light with a bit of weight sharing. Eyes can remain closed or open. Focus on your own breath, and then tune in to the ebb and flow of each other's breath. Let the movement freely grow a bit, but stay back-to-back, with only small movements. Listen to the small dance, and follow those barely visible movements.

Second Step

One partner stays sitting to provide a solid, but not rigid, vertical surface for the other. The sitter can support herself with arms on the floor, legs bent or straight. Gradually move more, exploring the back's surface, allowing energy and sensation.

The other slides, pushes into, rolls, rubs against that surface. Imagine you're a cat against a couch, a wild pig against a tree, or a bull against a fence. Try going upside down and giving additional weight, but stick primarily to a horizontal force.

Change roles.

Sit back to back again and slowly move away from each other until separate.

Third Step

Think with your back. Move through space with your back in the forefront of attention. Let it touch the floor, slide across the floor, and rise up again into space. Let breath deepen and spread. Breathe deeply into it, and allow it to spread in all directions. Arch forward and backward. Send limbs to probe space, relying on the back to initiate movement.

Fourth Step

Do a duet with the backs, but without touching. Imagine there are eyes on your back. Watch your partner approach and move away. Gradually touch, as if both backs would like to lightly kiss each other.

Fifth Step

One person dances by offering her back as steady supporter to a partner. The partner uses that back as a moving surface, giving a range of weight and touching with any part of her body. Essentially, one is a provider, the other a user. The provider receives the weight and moves with it, carefully staying connected.

Switch roles.

Switch roles again but without establishing who is doing what. Continue the contact duet while blurring roles.

MAGIC WANDS
Martin Keogh

Some Contacters avoid flying altogether. Going up on a partner's body increases the distance from the floor and the possibility of injury from falling. Falling is very much a part of the dance, and the more we practice the safe routes to the floor, the more prepared we are to handle the unexpected falls. Martin Keogh's exercises show us three ways to befriend the floor through controlled falls. The guidance he provides in helping us lower our supple body downward turns a potential for injury into surefire fun.

Martin Keogh has taught and performed Contact Improvisation since 1980. He regularly tours and has facilitated conferences for CI teachers on four continents. For his contribution to the development of Contact Improvisation he is listed in Who's Who in America.

When I teach, I often foment a sense of playfulness, especially during warm-ups. This animates the group and generates an ease of interaction between the students. Games can serve to create an atmosphere as well as teach the principles and techniques of the form.

I sometimes say there are three kinds of falls in Contact Improvisation: 1) The Folding Fall, 2) The Rolling Fall, and 3) The Long Fall.

In the Folding Fall the body creases and folds to the floor in the same way a scarf folds onto itself if you drop it straight down. The Rolling Fall has the body curling into a ball and rolling as it falls, like an orange rolling out of your hand. In the Long Fall the body organizes so that a lot of surface breaks the fall, as if you were letting a banana roll down its long edge.

It's not true that there are only three kinds of falls, but explaining it that way awakens the psyche for what it's about to learn.

To introduce the Folding Fall I use an exercise called "Crease Wands" that generates a lot of fun and laughter while teaching a skill. I used to call it "Crease Guns" until the Harry Potter books came out and the image of aggression was replaced by one of magic.

This structure is used as a warm-up, as an icebreaker, and as a mixer. It gets people laughing, energetic and interacting. It also helps break down inhibitions about touch, because the touch has narrowly defined parameters and a purpose.

Everyone starts by walking through the room. I tell them that their left hands are magic wands. If someone touches you with their wand, you have to try to swallow their fingers right at that part of the body where you are being touched. You try to fold and crease around the fingers.

As you crease locally, the other joints also crease, and you fold to the floor. Once you have reached the floor, the person removes the touch of the wand, and you return to walking. If the person accidentally tries to crease you with their right hand, they have to give you a shoulder massage.

After a while, I say that I was researching on the internet and Crease Wand 2.3 had just been released. Now you don't have to touch someone to make them fold to the floor, you can project the spell through the air by making a sound as you cast your spell. The person sending the spell keeps sending it until their recipient has reached the floor. With the addition of sounds, the feeling in the room becomes more exuberant.

Many variations have grown from these first two. Here are a few:

• When the person receives the spell, they jump into the air and then crease to the ground.

- They lift one foot and crease to the ground.
- You cast the spell at two people at once — you then jump, and the two people put their hands on your waist to help you fly higher and land softly.
- With a more advance group I might have you crease someone and that person flies at you for a short ride.

I then say that Apple has just come out with the Macintosh version of Crease Wands. Now when you cast a spell towards a place on someone, that is the spot on your body that you would like to have hugged. The person comes and hugs you there, waits till they feel a release pass through your body and then they gently twist, introducing a spiral in your body. This spiral creates creases at the joints that allows them to easily fold you down to the floor.

The next Macintosh version is to hug and then lift at that place, maybe even organizing under you enough to lift you right off the ground. After putting you down, they once again look for the creases, folding you softly to the floor.

This exercise teaches that a smooth painless way to move into the floor is to fold, and it shows us that we can initiate that folding from almost anywhere in the body. The use of the big muscles in the legs, repeatedly lowering to the floor and back up, brings us to an aerobic heart rate in preparation for dancing. Using the imagination with the magic wands and engaging the voice helps create a liveliness and ease of interaction. And out of the playfulness of this structure I have the satisfaction of discovering a new variation almost every time.

VESSEL IN A HAND
Brad Stoller

A challenge of Contact Improvisation is perceiving the body's natural flow and letting go to the momentum generated when we share weight and play with balance. We're so used to controlling ourselves, finding poise whenever possible, that we hesitate when we finally receive the okay to release our weight and follow the contours of jointly moving bodies. Brad Stoller has us consider our relationship to gravity. With us tuning in to feel the inner substance of our body, we can be more receptive to the subtle and not so subtle shifts of weight. Such shifts set us into motion and soften us to the moments of making contact. Letting go leads us into effortless dancing and spontaneity.

Brad Stoller is a certified Alexander Technique teacher and has a black belt in Aikido. He has been teaching and practicing Contact Improvisation since 1980. He lives in Central Virginia, where he writes plays and dances.

Imagine the floor as a large hand. Rest in it as it forms around you. Now let the hand gently move you. Feel yourself roll easily back and forth. Curl up in it. Rest. Let all your breath out.

Now fill up with fresh soft air from your toes to the top of your head. Breathe as if your whole body were lungs and every part of you could expand and contract, all the way down to the cells. Feel breath between your toes, beneath your fingernails, through your eyelids — all the places that hide in shadow. Feel your spaciousness.

Imagine that you're an empty vessel. Slowly fill about two-thirds with sand or metal filings or chocolate pudding. Let this substance shift inside you. Let it shift to the right or left. Feel that side of your body become heavy and the other side light. Feel it pour back and forth.

Slowly allow the empty side to float away from the floor. Continue this shift of substance inside you, and let it grow stronger, larger, more rhythmic and energetic. Then let the substance shift from upper to lower body, and allow it to roll you around. Feel the suspension you get when you allow the shift of the weight to continue its directional momentum even when the body has stopped. Experience the counterbalance of weight and direction like a boat riding in the waves. Then experience the potential energy of the falling weight before it falls. Catch it! Ride it!

Sit on the floor behind a partner. Bring your hands and forearms to your partner's head, neck, and upper back. Let the weight of your partner's head rest in your arms and hands, and gently roll it. Let it move all over your arms, and gently guide your partner to falling. Guide your partner all the way to the ground and then back up again to standing. Breathe. Switch roles.

DEFYING GRAVITY

Jayne Bernasconi

For many Contacters, the ultimate thrill is finding a site on the body that maximizes height and flight, rotating around a partner's shoulder or balancing from a head. Carelessly test the laws of gravity and the punishment can be bruising. The more we can familiarize ourselves with our feet aloft, the more we can relax into the moments of disorientation, when the floor and ceiling blur and our inner compass momentarily spins. In this exercise, Jayne Bernasconi, who sees a symbiotic relationship between Contact Improvisation and aerial dancing, leads Contacters into a comfort with height and aerialists into some of the principles of CI.

Jayne Bernasconi is the artistic director of Air Dance Bernasconi, an aerial dance company based in Baltimore. She teaches modern dance and choreography at Towson University and aerial arts such as low-flying trapeze and aerial yoga classes at Gerstung in Baltimore.

Defying gravity, flying through or just being suspended in space, is a feeling of pure joy and rapture. When dancing/flying, one of my goals is to blur the laws of gravity so that my body (and soul) can swoop upward and push through the spatial boundaries that are rarely explored in these dimensions. When flying through space, it is important to drop out of my head and let my body navigate space and time. Momentum takes the helm and acts as a magical tour guide. I'm always amazed at some of the feats that can be accomplished in the air during great contact dances.

Here are two warm-up exercises that will prepare you to discover your own laws of gravity-less dancing. The first exercise is based on solo and partner work. The second is based on working with a low flying trapeze as your contact partner.

Solo and Partner Work

Lie on the floor, eyes closed, and focus on the breath as it rises and falls. Take several slow breaths to settle into the floor, and then begin to put your mind in an altered state by imagining the ceiling as the floor and the floor as the ceiling. Your back is touching the ceiling instead of the floor, and your nose is pointing downward towards the floor. Feel the entire surface of your back stuck to the ceiling and the front surface of your body flowing with blood as it wants to pull you down to the floor. Begin to shift your weight by rolling very slowly (at a snail's pace) first to your side, and then your back, always keeping in mind the new relationship of ceiling and floor. Finish the roll on your back again. Take several minutes to initiate different body parts in a roll: hips, shoulders, head, feet.

Now with a partner, one person lies on his stomach and the other lies perpendicular to roll up and down her partner — always keeping in mind that the pull of gravity is over instead of below. Take turns being rolled on. Progress to a tabletop position. One partner is on his hands and feet for support while the other is exploring hanging shapes on her partners back, always reversing the pull of gravity in her mind upward. Moving slow is key to keeping your frame of mind in this altered state. As you progress to standing, let the dance unfold as you maintain the reversed ceiling/floor image.

Rolling Point Using a Low-Flying Trapeze

A double trapeze, or a single bar that can be lowered or raised according to need, is ideal for this exercise. The lowest bar should be approximately 1½ to 2 feet from the ground. You may want to experiment with the height of the bar, depending on personal preference.

Start by sitting on the floor grounded evenly on your sit bones, cross-legged under the trapeze. The first part of the exercise is done slowly, and the range of movement is small. Eyes are closed to sense how the body can move with the bar which is attached to lines (ropes) running upward to a fixed point of attachment in the ceiling. Place the bar under your armpits, and try to let your legs go along for the ride. As you begin to rock forward, backward and to each side, your weight shifts from armpits to your sit bones.

Feel how your weight falls into the bar under your arms and then catches in various positions. Now try hooking both elbows around the bar and moving the weight to your heels grounded into the floor, lifting up your hips and straightening your torso and legs. Most of your weight will be in your elbows and some in your feet as you begin falling in a circular motion. Next lie on your back on the floor, and place the ankles over the bar. Lift your lower back and buttocks from the floor as your upper back, arms and head stay grounded. Swing the feet from side to side, and feel the gentle rocking motion of your spine. Keep your eyes closed, and experiment by moving the bar from the feet to the armpits to the elbows and attaching various body parts to roll through the bar, keeping your body attached to the ground and bar. Then place the bar in the crease of your hips, belly facing the floor, and feel the weight of your body hanging over the bar. Your hands and feet will touch the floor. Move your weight around, shifting the rolling point to your hips. When beginners first learn how to release their weight into a bar, such as in a hip hang, they often feel pain because their muscles are tensed. Subtle shifting and releasing of the muscles will soften the pain and lengthen the spine. Release, and breathe.

Now let the bar become your partner as your movement becomes improvised. Shift and roll from your belly to back, over, under, around and through the bar. The bar is low to the ground, allowing you to stay grounded on your sit bones and knees or feet, as you push and pull the bar with various body parts. Once you feel comfortable exploring your improv, move the bar up to about chin height or approximately 5 feet from the ground. Stand up and place your hands on the bar as wide apart as possible, wrapping your thumbs around the bar, and then let your weight sink into the floor. Do not let your shoulders come up to your ears. Keep your feet firmly planted into the ground and start stretching and pulling your body like taffy. As you are "pulling taffy" begin to imagine threads running from your solar plexus to the trapeze line's point of attachment into the ceiling. As you move and roll to explore your weight in your hands on the bar and feet on the ground, stay connected with the lines from your belly to the ceiling that guide you through your dance. If you're twisted or turned so your navel is facing downward, the thread comes through your back up to the ceiling. This image of being attached and connected to an upward point helps to keep your weight lifted and flowing freely through the lower torso.

DOWN TO GO UP MIXER
*Kristin Horrigan**

There are a number of ways to find yourself rising into the air and onto your partner's body. One of the challenges to the lifter is finding a way to hoist up your partner that is both smoothly executed and avoids undue muscle strain and weight on any one joint. Kristin Horrigan urges us to take advantage of the upward springing of a partner to accomplish a lift that doesn't require brute strength. Her method contains a secondary benefit as well; it simultaneously enhances the height our partner reaches. Contact Improvisation is often about taking advantage of the body's natural trajectories, and this exercise cues us in to recognizing the invitations that lead easily to changing altitude.

Kristin Horrigan is an improviser, choreographer, performer and teacher based in Northampton, Massachusetts, who teaches CI in colleges and community settings.

Begin standing. As a warm-up for this exercise, find the spring in your legs, bend to and straightening your knees. Take this into the air with some soft jumps, feeling how your knees bending cushion your landing and provide power for your next. Listen to the sound of your jumping. On the next landing, try to land silently by rolling through your feet from ball to heel.

Now find a partner. One person will stand close behind the other and place her hands on her partner's hips. The person in front will take

*This exercise was developed in collaboration with Spirit Joseph and inspired by exercises from Andrew Harwood.

a few jumps, while the job of the person behind is simply to track the jumping motion.

The next step will be for the person in back to add a little upward force as her partner is going up. (When you reach for his hips, be sure to put your hands on the bones of his pelvis rather than on the soft, squishy flesh just above. It's a more effective and feels much better on his belly!) As you track your partner's pelvis going up, add in force gradually and give your partner a chance to soar at the top of the jump. (It's also nice to offer your partner a little resistance on the way down so that he doesn't come crashing to the floor.) The person jumping can increase the feeling of flight by sweeping his arms out to the side and upward with each jump.

How might this happen in the dance? We could wait for someone to jump and hope that we're in a good place to provide a boost during the flight. Or we could signal to our partner that it's time to jump by pressing down into his pelvis, causing him to bend his knees. This loads up the springs of his legs and lets him know that we're in position to assist his jump. *Down to go up.* Try some more jumps like those we just did, but this time the partner in back will initiate. The partner in front can just stand and wait, listening for the signal.

The next variation takes our jumping into different directions. If I push down *and to the side* when I load up my partner's legs, I take his center of mass off balance. Thus when he jumps he'll travel to the side that I directed. We can also do this to the front and back.

Try this with the whole group. Begin circulating through the room. At any moment you can stop and wait or you can approach someone who is waiting and give them a "down to go up" signal.

Now what happens if I lean off-center as I push down into my partner? My partner must push back into me (or else be pushed through space). When he jumps, if he keeps pushing into me, and jumps towards me, he will push me back over my center. I must keep my contact with him, both through my hands and through whatever parts of my body are touching him (probably my shoulder and head). This allows me to channel some of his weight down through my skeleton so that my arms are not doing all of the work. The flying partner can help make the lift feel easy by extending his arms upward on the way up and reaching his torso in the direction of the jump. He should treat his flight as a potential solo journey, taking responsibility for finding a landing, rather than relying on me to support him entirely. As the lifter, I will move my feet during the lift, pivoting to follow the arc of my partner's jump, and perhaps extending that arc by traveling in space. Try this exercise first with a partner of similar size.

We can also do this kind of lifting without using our hands. A simple version is to lift your partner onto your back, so that he is balanced with his belly on your pelvis and his body perpendicular to yours. To come into this lift, stand one to two feet in front of your partner with your body turned 90 degrees to the side, and then lunge off balance into your partner, leaning your pelvis against his. Let your body slide down your partner a bit both to bring your body below his center of mass and to encourage him to bend his knees a little. As you slide, spiral your torso open to make a broader contact point between your back and your partner's pelvis. The flying partner should reach his arms up over his head and send his body into a horizontal position as he pushes your pelvis back towards your balance point (where your weight is between your two feet). Depending on how much force your partner puts into his jump, following the arc of the lift might take you past your balance point into a suspension on one leg. To avoid falling, pivot on this leg and set your partner down on his feet. (An added twist to this lift is for the person you approach to lift to wrap his arms under your torso and free leg and, by standing up and rocking back, to lift you. He can then rock forward again, and you can continue into the lift you had planned.)

To finish, open things up by moving in and out of short dances while playing with these ideas of lifting, with and without your hands, using the signaling system of "down to go up." Let yourself experiment with new variations. See if you can find ways to land from flight in an off-balance position, leaning into your partner. This creates an opening for another lift to happen right away, alternating who is the lifter and who is taking flight.

SAYING NO

Brenton Cheng

Contact Improvisation is awkward when we find ourselves reluctant to accept an invitation to move in a certain way. "Going with the flow" is an enticing catch-phrase, yet there are times when the flow introduced is not mutually acceptable. Discovering and respecting limits and boundaries is imperative to the dance staying safely grounded and satisfying. A partner can voice an emphatic "No," if direct-ness is needed. Brenton Cheng's exercises show us how to decline an invitation through movement, a rejection that doesn't end the dance but instead gives the dance a creative twist that ultimately feeds back into a mutually agreeable flow.

Brenton Cheng came from long-distance running, fell into martial arts, and from there tumbled into Contact Improvisation and contemporary dance. He teaches in France and Russia and is based in Oakland, California.

Often I find an idea in the air that in contact, one must say yes to everything, and must go with the flow, must accept everything, including everything that is done to you. What I think is sometimes missing is the idea that you can say no while still agreeing to partici-pate in and be present with the dance. Therefore, I like to engage the creative no as a way not only to set boundaries when needed, but also to enliven the dance by giving voice to an often neglected polarity. With that in mind, here are three sets of exercises, done in duets:

Part 1

"A" gives physical impulses to "B," whose body moves in response. When giving impulses, "A" feels the connection from her own center to the place of contact with "B," which can be anywhere on "B." "B" is "agreeable" in his body, going with each impulse from "A" in a light, available way, rather than being completely passive. So, "A" moves "B" around the space.

Part 2

"A" gives physical impulses to "B," as before. "B," this time, can choose to be agreeable, or in any given moment, he may choose to refuse to move in the direction of the impulse, resisting in place. He may then decide to resume being agreeable. When refusing to move, "A" is encouraged to be jovially stubborn, that is, to still be fully engaged in the interaction, even while saying no.

Part 3

For a short time, "B" plays with saying "No" to every impulse that "A" gives, either by disappearance or resistance.

No by Disappearance

"A" and "B" stand facing each other. "A" reaches out to push or pull "B" anywhere on "B"'s body except directly through "B"'s center. As soon as "B" feels the touch and direction of force, she immediately releases the place where the force is being applied so that "A"'s push or pull has nothing to resist against and flows right by. "B" may need to twist in place or bend in the joints around where the force was applied in order to facilitate the evasion. This exercise is similar to the Tai Chi image of the sparrow that could not jump out of the master's hand, because his hand was so released that the sparrow had nothing to push off against.

For a vocal or theatrical addition, a coy "no" spoken by "B" when melting under each touch adds to the spirit of the game. This can be followed with doing the exercise for 30 seconds at high speed.

No by Resistance

"A" and "B" stand facing each other. "A" reaches out to push or pull somewhere on "B." "B" lets the touch land but then resists the impulse by pressing against it, refusing to move, using her connection up from the ground, through her center, and to the point of contact, providing the strength of resistance. Adding a fiery, robust "No!" (think pirates) seems to work pretty well here. Again, one can end with a 30 second version of the exercise at high speed.

When working with support structures for lifting, the practice of compassionate dumping is often helpful. If "B" is lifting "A," then B can practice different ways of dumping "A," while at the same time offering body surfaces for A to friction slide down or limbs to help slow the fall. Or not. This practice not only gives "B" options for releasing undesired weight to the ground; it also gives both partners a chance to practice finding pathways in sudden survival moments.

KOAN DANCING

Carolyn Stuart

Abandoning habit and embracing improvisation is an acquired skill. Once we step onto the floor to meet the fleeting moment, we find out to what degree habit runs everything from the way we think to the way we move. To increase awareness of the creative potential of the moment and the infinite variations of connecting with our partner, it is helpful to play with unusual methods to kick us out of familiar patterns. Carolyn Stuart's exercise borrows from the Zen tradition of using koans to awaken us to the workings of our mind and to the hidden realities that lie everywhere. "In Zen, a koan is a formulation, in baffling language, pointing to ultimate Truth," explains Phillip Kapleau Roshi in The Three Pillars of Zen. *"Koans cannot be solved by recourse to a logical reasoning but only awakening a deeper level of the mind beyond the discursive intellect." Through the brevity and abstraction of her written lines, she challenges us to find deeper truths in our dancing than what we may customarily abide by.*

Carolyn Stuart is the cocreator of the Touchmonkey perspective of Contact Improvisation. She teaches and performs worldwide, offering intensives that explore the relationship of autonomy and union on and off the dance floor.

> Pick a koan and together dance out its meaning.
> Any koan, find one or make one up, any one.
> Hold it. Dance it.
> Tell each other the story of what happens.
> Equal time, equal respect.
> Witness yourselves receive.
> Watch the next koan reveal itself.
> Dance it. Tell it.
> Look for who does the telling

and from where the telling speaks.
Dance again.

My bones are your bones are my bones.
One body, two minds.

Knowing has no words.
It is I that I can know.
It is I that must show up
to voice the question
for what is not known,
which cannot yet speak.

Dance again.

Koan again to occupy the mind
so that the body being does the telling.
Curiosity only. Practice only.
Practice changes the practitioner.
The unending unfolding mystery
dancing on,
one koan to the next
gathering what is as it is,
is enough.

Care who shows up to dance.
Get to know them well.

Glossary

balance— equilibrium; a swaying or stepping away from and regaining equilibrium; equal weight toward and away from a contact point

centered— a state of physiological and emotional balance and integration

Contact Improvisation— a partnered dance form, developed by Steve Paxton, that relies on improvised movements and continual physical contact

contact point— pivotal to Contact Improvisation, sites on the body where partners physically connect

counterbalance— shared balance with partners opposing each other with equal weight or force

effortless effort— a balance between necessary exertion and minimal exertion that propels the dance easily

flying— rotating atop a partner's shoulders or hips with feet off the floor

gap— a period of physical or psychic confusion within the dance, often a harbinger of surprise

grounding— a state of balance and integration free of stress that emphasizes a solid, mutually supported relationship with the earth

jam— a loosely structured gathering for Contact Improvisation

jammers— the dancers who gather for Contact Improvisation at a jam

kinesphere— the immediate space around a body

kinesthesia— the sense of the body's weight, position, and movement

letting go— a surrendering to present circumstances; releasing will into the flow of the moment

listening (also active listening)— sensing you and your partner's subtle and obvious activity; paying careful attention to shifts in weight, muscle tension, balance, and strength

moving from center— movements arising out of centeredness and balance

proprioception— the ability to sense the movement and spatial orientation that arise from stimuli within the body

releasing— letting go of tension and unnecessary holding in deep and superficial tissue

rolling point of contact— the constantly traveling contact point across partners' bodies

sloughing— sliding down or up the body of your partner

Small Dance— an awareness exercise developed by Steve Paxton that focuses on the minute activity of the body most noticeable during stillness

somatics— the study of the body with an emphasis on the mind-body connection

weight sharing— leaning with weight into the contact point; a mutual relationship of support

Appendix A:
Setting Up a Weekly
Contact Improvisation Jam

Many factors contribute to establishing and sustaining a regional jam. Jams with the best attendance and longevity are typically located in a sizeable metropolitan area and rely on several core folks sharing responsibility. The specifics of every jam differ: A landlord may provide a dance space for free; the meeting may take place once a month rather than weekly; those traveling a distance may need to carpool. Check with participants to find out what works for them.

1. **Find a space.** A floor that is wood or vinyl surface (often called Marley) is best. Avoid concrete floors or linoleum floors on top of concrete. Possible sites include a university or private dance studio, a yoga center, an art center, a church, or an old warehouse. Aim for a central location.

2. **Decide on a meeting time.** Intend the session to last 2 to 3 hours. The meeting time may change once a group is established; however, it is best to keep the same time each week, especially when initiating a jam. Weekends work for some; others prefer weeknights. Consider offering jams at two times if the population is large enough to sustain two jams. If the time alternates from week to week, keep the change to a minimum, for instance, only two times monthly. Send out weekly reminders of the meeting day and time.

3. **Pay rent.** Estimate the number of attendees anticipated and divide the space rental fee accordingly. Collect money weekly.

4. **Hire a teacher.** If jamming is new to your region, arrange for a Contact Improvisation teacher to lead a class. The teacher can guide participants skillfully and safely into the dance. Consider regular classes, perhaps once a month or four times a year, as a way for jammers to improve their skills.

5. **Get the word out.** Invite participants by word of mouth, flyers at dance departments and studios, yoga and martial art studios, health food stores, and emails to appropriate groups. Lead a class at a dance or bodywork studio to introduce the dance to newcomers. Consider an events listing in a local newspaper. List your jam at contactimprov.net or another appropriate site. Create a website.

6. **Share information.** In an opening circle at the start of the jam, welcome participants and exchange names. Or end each jam with a closing circle. You might talk about skills, injuries, talking while dancing, the use of live music, jams in other regions, classes, or related events.

7. **Stay in communication.** Establish an email list for announcements and communications.

8. **Lead a warm-up.** Get someone to lead a short warm-up at the start of every jam. A warm-up gets jammers focused on their body and reduces chatter.

9. **Share responsibilities.** Avoid the burnout that can accompany one person being in charge of collecting money, holding the key, sweeping the floor, sending out communications, and leading warm-ups by getting several folks to assume specific duties.

10. **Hang out.** Consider periodic venues to socialize outside the jam, such as going out for lunch, having a potluck, or attending a dance concert.

11. **Cultivate creativity.** Be ambitious and collaborate on a dance performance or multimedia show.

Appendix B:
Resources

Recommended Reading

Contact Improvisation

Contact Quarterly, P.O. Box 603, Northampton, MA 01061; www.contactquar
terly.com; email: info@contactquarterly.com. This magazine, edited by
Nancy Stark Smith, is the primary source for articles and information on
Contact Improvisation and related movement practices.

*Contact Quarterly's Sourcebook: Collected Writings and Graphics from CQ 1975–
1992*, Contact Editions, MA, 1997. A great collection of the influential
writings from the early years of the magazine.

Proximity, P.O. Box 1065, North Fitzroy, Victoria, Australia 3068; http://prox
imity.slightly.net; email: proximity@slightly.net. Not nearly as packed as
Contact Quarterly, each issue contains valuable articles about CI and information on events in Australia.

Sharing the Dance, Cynthia Novak. Madison: University of Wisconsin Press,
1991. A well researched account of CI's early years and its emergence into
modern dance.

The Art of Waiting: Essays on Contact Improvisation, Martin Keogh, www.martin.
keogh.com. Keogh's metaphorically rich book provides valuable insights
for those wanting to hone their CI practice.

Bodywork

Body Stories: A Guide to Experiential Anatomy, Andrea Olsen. Hanover, NH:
University Press of New England, 1994. A step-by-step guide to understanding and telling the stories of our body.

Bone, Breath, Gesture: Practices of Embodiment, Don Hanlon Johnson. Berkeley,
CA: North Atlantic, 1995. A valuable introduction to the writings of

different healing modalities written by founders like Ida Rolf and Mary Whitehouse.

Dance and the Lived Body: A Descriptive Aesthetics, Sonda Horton Fraleigh. Pittsburgh: University of Pittsburgh Press, 1987 (reprinted 1996). An insightful reflection and analysis of the moving body, with an emphasis on phenomenology.

Job's Body: A Handbook for Bodywork, Deane Juhan. Barrytown, NY: Station Hill, 2002. Often considered a must-have book by bodyworkers, this is a detailed book on anatomy and its connection to the physiology and psychology of touch.

Wisdom of the Moving Body: An Introduction to Body-Mind-Centering, Linda Hartley. Berkeley, CA: North Atlantic Books, 1995. A system-by-system presentation of Bonnie Bainbridge Cohen's somatic approach to moving.

General Reading

The Anthropology of Performance, Victor Turner. New York: PAJ, 1986. Also *From Ritual to Theater: The Human Seriousness of Play*, New York: PAJ, 1982. These provocative books situate common conceptions of dance into a broad anthropological frame and can be inspirational in generating new ideas for performance.

Democracy's Body: Judson Dance Theater, 1962–1964, Sally Banes. This 1983 book, reprinted by Duke University Press in 1993, chronicles the boon of New York's experimental art scene, which provided the creative ground for Contact Improvisation's eventual founding.

Moving History/Dancing Cultures: A Dance History Reader, Ann Cooper Albright, ed. Middletown, CT: Wesleyan University Press, 2001. A collection of essays about dance traditions from around the world.

Taken By Surprise: A Dance Improvisation Reader, Ann Cooper Albright and David Gere, eds. Middletown, CT: Wesleyan University Press, 2003. This diverse collection of essays, which includes writings by Steve Paxton and Nancy Stark Smith, elevates improvisation to its rightful place as an illuminating mode of performance.

CONTACT IMPROVISATION VIDEO

Fall After Newton, P.O. Box 22, E. Charleston, VT 05833; www.contactquar terly.com/vd/vd.html; email: videoda@together.net. This video on the first 11 years of Contact Improvisation is written and narrated by Steve Paxton.

Videoda carries several other historic Contact Improvisation videos for rent or purchase.

WEBSITES

Below are sources for finding local jams, classes and retreats.

In the United States

www.contactimprov.net — This site is the main hub for CI jams, classes, articles, and more. The emphasis is on the United States, but it contains extensive international resources as well.

http://contactimprov.com/worldjammap.html — This site is another good international source for jams and classes.

http://contactimprov.com/texas.html — Austin, Texas

geocities.com/contactimprovboston — Boston, MA

www.eastcoastjam — East Coast

www.glacierdancer.com — Great Lakes and Midwest

www.harbinjam.org — Harbin Springs, CA

http://www.contactimprovla.com — Los Angeles, CA

www.moabjam.com — Moab UT

http://www.movingarts.net/ci-jam.html — San Diego, CA

www.seattlecontactimprovisation.com — Seattle, WA

www.improvfestival.com — Washington DC

www.wccif.com — West Coast

International

proximity.slightly.net/links.htm — Australia

www.inntanz.com — Austria

www.contactimpro.org — Canada

www.kimpro.dk/index.htm — Denmark

www.ateliercontact.fr.tc — France

www.contact-improvisation.de — Germany

www.contactfestival.de — Freiburg, Germany

http://jamcontact.7h.com — Greece

www.contactil.org — Israel

www.contactfestival.it — Italy

http://www.geocities.com/amsterdamjam — Netherlands

plombir.web.ur.ru — Russia
http://www.tanzelarija.org — Sarajevo
http://www.movimiento-bcn.org — Spain
www.contactimprovisation.ch — Switzerland and Europe
contactimprovisation.co.uk — United Kingdom

Notes

PREFACE

1. There are videos as well, most notably *Fall After Newton* and *Chute*. For a complete list of recommended titles, see Appendix B: Resources.

CHAPTER 1

1. Steve Paxton. Interview, September 2, 1998.

2. Steve Paxton. Email, November 15, 1998.

3. For further information on this topic, Cynthia Novak's *Sharing the Dance* provides an extensive study on CI history and its influences. Sally Bane's *Democracy's Body: Judson Dance Theater, 1962–1964* presents great detail on the New York art scene.

4. Steve Paxton. Interview, December 3, 2001.

5. Steve Paxton. Interview, November 15, 1998.

6. Steve Paxton. "Contact Improvisation," *The Drama Review*, Vol. 19 (March 1975): 40–41.

7. Ibid., 40.

8. Nancy Stark Smith. Interview, April 2, 2002.

9. Danny Lepkoff. "A Definition," *Contact Quarterly*, Vol. 2, no. 4 (Summer 1977).

10. Steve Paxton. Interview, December 3, 2001.

CHAPTER 2

1. Ruth Zaporah. "(Not) A Bag of Tricks," *Contact Quarterly*, Vol. 12, no. 1 (1987): 34.

2. Mary Oliver. *New and Selected Poems: Volume One.* Boston: Beacon, 2004.

3. Nancy Stark Smith. "Taking No for an Answer," *Contact Quarterly*. Vol. 12, no. 2 (1987): 3.

4. Steve Paxton. "Improvisation Is ..." *Contact Quarterly*, Vol. 12, no. 1 (1987): 16.

5. Martin Keogh. "The Earth is Breathing You," unpublished article.

6. Karen Nelson. "Interview: Lisa Nelson and Olga Sorokina," *Contact Quarterly*, Vol. 27, no. 2 (2002): 71–72.

7. Curt Siddall. "Reflections on Contact Improvisation," *Contact Quarterly*, Vol. 23, no. 1 (1998): 27–29.

CHAPTER 3

1. Howard Gardner. *Frames of Mind: The Theory of Multiple Intelligences* (New York: Basic, 1983).

2. Maurice Merleau-Ponty. *The Pri-*

macy of Perception (Evanston, IL: Northwestern University Press, 1964), 162.

3. Ann Cooper Albright. *Choreographing Difference: The Body and Identity in Contemporary Dance* (Hanover, NH: University Press of New England, 1977), 47.

4. Helene Gronda. "Practicing the Body: Contact Improvisation and Body Awareness" (unpublished paper, 2000), 1.

5. Sondra Fraleigh. Email, May 19, 2002.

6. As quoted in Cynthia Novack, *Sharing the Dance* (Madison: University of Wisconsin Press, 1990), 164.

7. Ron Estes. Interview, July 7, 2002.

8. Breanna Rowland. Class journal, 2001.

9. Ranjabati Sircar. "Contacting Cultures: Zen, Contact, & Classical Indian Dance," *Contact Quarterly* (Winter/Spring 1997), 14.

10. Gloria Lee. Interview, September 3, 2002.

11. Richard Aviles. Interview, July 7, 2002.

12. K. Interview, March 23, 2002.

Chapter 4

1. "Government Support for the Arts: Federal, State and Local, 1994–2005." Americans for the Arts, www.AmericansForTheArts.org, August 2, 2005.

2. Sherry B. Shapiro. *Pedagogy and the Politics of the Body: A Critical Praxis* (New York: Garland, 1999), 104.

3. Jane Desmond, ed. *Dancing Desires: Choreographing Sexualities On and Off the Stage* (Madison: University of Wisconsin Press, 2001), 32.

4. Ann Cooper Albright. "Strategic Abilities: Negotiating the Disabled Body in Dance." *Moving History* (Middletown, CT: Wesleyan University Press, 2001), 56.

5. Maia Scott. Email, January 18, 1999.

6. Ibid.

7. Ron Estes. Interview, July 7, 2002.

8. Kristin Horrigan. Interview, July 7, 2002.

9. Thich Nhat Hanh. *The Heart of the Buddha's Teaching* (Berkeley, CA: Parallax, 1998).

10. Vladimir Angelov. Interview, September 18, 2002.

11. Don Hanlon Johnson. *Body: Recovering Our Sensual Wisdom* (Berkeley, CA: North Atlantic, 1992), 14.

12. Andrew Wass. Email, February 25, 2002.

13. Johnson, 66–7.

Chapter 5

1. There have been numerous studies on touch-deprived infants and adults, but a good source of information is Deane Juhan's *Job's Body: Handbook for Bodywork* (Barrytown, NY: Station Hill, 1998).

2. Juhan. 83.

3. Jennifer Stanger. Interview, April, 14, 2002.

4. Juhan, 29.

5. Richard Gerber. *Vibrational Medicine: The #1 Handbook of Subtle-Energy Therapies* (Rochester, VT: Bear and Company, 2001), 43.

6. Robert Ochsman. "Readings on the Scientific Basis of Bodywork and Movement Therapies: The Connective Tissue and Myofascial Systems," *Somatics*, www.somatics.de/Oshman.htm, August 3, 2002.

7. Ashley Montagu. *Growing Young* (New York: McGraw-Hill, 1981).

8. Neuroscientist Candace Pert has adopted the word "bodymind" to emphasize the inextricable link between body and mind, seeing them as a loop with neither beginning nor end. See Candace Pert's *Molecules of Emotion* (New York: Scribner, 1997).

9. Richard Aviles. Interview, July 3, 2002.

10. Johann Wolfgang. *Goethe's Faust*:

The Prologues and Part One: Trans. Baylor Taylor. Collier, 1962.

11. Joseph Campbell. *Primitive Mythology* (New York: Viking, 1969), 21–22.

12. Jean Houston. "Africa, Music and the Making of Soul." Homepage http://www.jeanhouston.org/lectures/africalecture.html. Accessed December 26, 2002.

13. Alicia Grayson. Interview, July 3, 2002.

14. Shakti Andrea Smith. Interview, July 3, 2002.

15. Mindell identifies channels, or ways of receiving information, as follows: body feeling or proprioception, visual, auditory, movement or kinesthesia, relationship, and world. See Arnold Mindell, *Working on Yourself Alone: Inner Dreambody Work* (New York: Penguin Arkana, 1990), 23–4.

16. Deborah Hay. *My Body, The Buddhist* (Hanover, NH: University Press of New England, 2000), xii.

17. Lynn Stephens. Interview, July 3, 2002.

18. Mihaly Csikszentmihaly. *Flow: The Psychology of Optimal Experience* (New York: HarperPerennial, 1991).

19. Holger Kalweit. *Shamans, Healers, and Medicine Men.* (Boston: Shambhala, 1987), 83.

CHAPTER 6

1. *American Heritage Dictionary of the English Language*, 4th ed. (New York: Houghton Mifflin, 2000).

2. Linda Hartley. *Wisdom of the Body Moving: An Introduction to Body-Mind Centering* (Berkeley, CA: North Atlantic, 1989), 124.

3. Howard Gardner. *Frames of Mind: The Theory of Multiple Intelligences* (New York: Basic, 1983).

4. Karen Knight. Interview, April 14, 2002.

5. Steven Harris. Interview, October 17, 2002.

6. Joe Tranquillo. Interview, October 17, 2002.

7. Susan Singer. Interview, April 14, 2002.

8. Cynthia Carter-Rounds. Interview, April 14, 2002.

9. Carolyn Stuart. Interview, February 2, 2003.

10. From *The Different Drum: Community-Making and Peace* by M. Scott Peck. Copyright © 1987 by M. Scott Peck, M.D., P.C. Reprinted by permission of Simon and Schuster Adult Publishing Group.

11. Suzi Gablik. *The Reenchantment of Art* (New York: Thames and Hudson, 1991), 114.

12. Victor Turner. *From Ritual to Theater: The Human Seriousness of Play* (New York: PAJ, 1982), 104–107.

13. Camille Paglia. "How Can Dance Education Compete with the Power of Media?" *Dance Magazine*, July 2005, 46.

Bibliography

Albright, Ann Cooper. *Choreographing Difference: The Body and Identity in Contemporary Dance.* Hanover, NH: University Press of New England, 1977.

_____. *Moving History/Dancing Cultures: A Dance History Reader.* Middletown, CT: Wesleyan University Press, 2001.

_____. and David Gere. *Taken by Surprise: A Dance Improvisation Reader.* Middletown, CT: Wesleyan University Press, 2003.

Banes, Sally. *Democracy's Body: Judson Dance Theater, 1962–1964.* Ann Arbor: UMI Research Press, 1983.

_____. "Steve Paxton: Physical Things." *Dance Scope*, Vol. 13, no. 2–3 (1979).

Campbell, Joseph. *Primitive Mythology.* New York: Viking, 1969.

Csikszentmihaly, Mihaly. *Flow: The Psychology of Optimal Experience.* New York: Harper Perennial, 1991.

Desmond, Jane. *Meaning in Motion: New Cultural Studies of Dance.* Durham, NC: Duke University Press, 1997.

_____, ed. *Dancing Desires: Choreographing Sexualities on and Off the Stage.* Madison: University of Wisconsin Press, 2001.

Dey, Misri Deitch. "Contact in Calcutta," *Contact Quarterly* Vol. 26, no. 2 (1998): 12–13.

Foster, Susan. *Corporealities: Dancing, Knowledge and Culture and Power.* New York: Routledge, 1995.

_____. *Dances That Describe Themselves: The Improvised Choreography of Richard Bull.* Middletown, CT: Wesleyan University Press, 2002.

Fraleigh, Sondra. "Consciousness Matters." *Dance Research Journal*, Vol. 32, no. 1 (Summer 2000).

_____. *Dance and the Lived Body.* Pittsburgh: University of Pittsburgh Press, 1987.

_____. *Dancing Identity: Metaphysics in Motion.* Pittsburgh: University of Pittsburgh Press, 2004.

Franko, Mark. *Dancing Modernism/Performing Politics.* Bloomington: Indiana University Press, 1995.

Gablik, Suzi. *The Reenchantment of Art*. New York: Thames and Hudson, 1991.

Gardner, Howard. *Frames of Mind: The Theory of Multiple Intelligences*. New York: Basic, 1983.

Gerber, Richard. *Vibrational Medicine: The #1 Handbook of Subtle-Energy Therapies*. Rochester, VT: Bear and Company, 2001.

Goellner, Ellen, and Jacqueline Shea Murphy. *Bodies of the Text: Dance as Theory, Literature as Dance*. New Brunswick, NJ: Rutgers University Press, 1995.

Goethe, Johann Wolfgang. *Goethe's Faust: The Prologues and Part One*. Trans. Baylard Taylor. Collier, 1962.

Gronda, Hellene. *Practicing the Body: Contact Improvisation and Body Awareness*. Unpublished ms.

Hanh, Thich Nhat. *The Heart of the Buddha's Teaching*. Berkeley, CA: Parallax, 1998.

Halprin, Anna. *Moving Toward Life: Five Decades of Transformational Dance*. Middletown, CT: Wesleyan University Press, 1995.

Hartley, Linda. *Wisdom of the Body Moving: An Introduction to Body-Mind Centering*. Berkeley, CA: North Atlantic, 1989.

Hay, Deborah. *My Body, The Buddhist*. Hanover, NH: University Press of New England, 2000.

Highwater, Jamake. *Dance: Rituals of Experience*. Highstown, NJ: Dance Horizons/Princeton Book Company, 1992.

Houston, Jean. "Africa, Music and the Making of Soul." Homepage http://www.jeanhouston.org/lectures/africalecture.html. Accessed December 26, 2002.

Johnson, Don Hanlon. *Body: Recovering Our Sensual Wisdom*. Berkeley, CA: North Atlantic, CA, 1992.

Juhan, Deane. *Job's Body: Handbook for Bodywork*. Barrytown, NY: Station Hill, 1998.

Kalweit, Holger. *Shamans, Healers, and Medicine Men*. Boston: Shambhala, 1987.

Keogh, Martin. *The Earth is Breathing You*. Unpublished article.

Klein, Anne Carolyn. *Meeting the Great Bliss Queen: Buddhists, Feminists, and the Art of the Self*. Boston: Beacon, 1995.

Lakoff, George, and Mark Johnson. *Philosophy in the Flesh: The Embodied Mind and Its Challenge to Western Thought*. New York: Basic, NY 1999.

Laughlin, Charles D., John McManus, and Eurgene d'Aquili. *Brain, Symbol and Experience: Toward a Neurophenomenology of Human Consciousness*. Boston: Shambhala, 1990.

Lepkoff, Danny. "A Definition," *Contact Quarterly*, Vol. 2, no. 4 (Summer 1977).

Luger, Eleanor Rachel. "A Contact Improvisation Primer." *Dance Scope*, Vol. 12, no. 1 (Fall/Winter).

Merleau-Ponty, Maurice. *The Primacy of Perception.* Evanston, IL: Northwestern University Press, 1978.

Mindell, Arnold. *Working on Yourself Alone: Inner Dreambody Work.* New York: Penguin/Arkana, 1990.

Montagu, Ashley. *Growing Young.* New York: McGraw-Hill, 1981.

Nachmanovitch, Stephen. *Free Play: The Power of Improvisation in Life and the Arts.* Los Angeles: Jeremy Tarcher, 1990.

Nelson, Karen. "Interview: Lisa Nelson and Olga Sorokina." *Contact Quarterly,* Vol. 27, no. 2 (2002): 71–72.

Novack, Cynthia J. *Sharing the Dance.* Madison: University of Wisconsin Press, 1990.

O'Brien, Katrina T. "The Social Construction of the Experiential Self: A Look at Dance and the Discourse of the Bodyself and Embodiment." Unpublished thesis, Middlebury College, April 21, 2000.

Ochsman, Robert. "Readings on the Scientific Basis of Bodywork and Movement Therapies: The Connective Tissue and Myofascial Systems." In *Somatics,* http://www.somatics.de/Oshman.htm. Accessed August 3, 2002.

Ochsman, Robert, and Candice Pert. *Energy Medicine: The Scientific Basis for Bioenergetic Medicine.* London: Churchhill Livingstone, 2000.

Oliver, Mary. *New and Selected Poems: Volume One.* Boston: Beacon, 2004.

Paglia, Camille. "How Can Dance Education Compete with the Power of Media?" *Dance Magazine,* July 2005.

Parviainen, Jaana. "Bodily Knowledge: Epistemological Reflections on Dance." *Dance Research Journal,* Vol. 34, no. 1 (Summer 2002).

Paxton, Steve. "Contact Improvisation." *The Drama Review,* Vol. 19 (March 1975).

_____. Personal interview. September 2, 1998.

_____. Personal interview. December 3, 2001.

_____. Email. November 15, 1998.

Peck, M. Scott. *The Different Drum: Community-Making and Peace.* New York: Simon and Schuster, 1987.

Pert, Candace. *Molecules of Emotion.* New York: Scribner, 1997.

Schechner, Richard. *The Future of Ritual: Writings on Culture and Performance.* New York: Routledge, 1993.

Shapiro, Sherry B. *Pedagogy and the Politics of the Body: A Critical Praxis.* New York: Garland, 1999.

Sheets-Johnston, Maxine. *The Primacy of Movement.* Philadelphia: John Benjamins, 1999.

Siddall, Curt. "Reflections on Contact Improvisation." *Contact Quarterly,* Vol. 23, no. 1 (1998): 27–29.

Smith, Nancy Stark. Personal interview. April 2, 2002.

_____. "Taking No for an Answer." *Contact Quarterly*, Vol. 12, no. 2 (1987): 3.

Turner, Victor. "Body, Brain, and Culture." *Zygon*, Vol. 18, no. 3 (1983).

_____. *From Ritual to Theatre: The Human Seriousness of Play.* New York: PAJ, 1982.

Ueshiba, Morihei. *The Art of Peace: Teachings of the Founder of Aikido.* (Trans. and comp. J. Stevens). Boston: Shambala, 1992.

Zaporah, Ruth. "(Not) A Bag of Tricks." *Contact Quarterly*, Vol. 12, no. 1 (1987), 34.

Index